UNSINKABLE

UNSINKABLE

My Untold Story

SILKEN LAUMANN

with Sylvia Fraser

HarperCollinsPublishersLtd

Unsinkable
Copyright © 2014 by Silken Laumann.
All rights reserved.

Published by HarperCollins Publishers Ltd

First Edition

Care has been taken to trace ownership of copyright material contained in this book.
The publisher will gladly receive any information that will enable it to update any
reference or credit line in subsequent editions.

All photos appear courtesy of the author except where otherwise noted.
On insert page 8, the photo by Beth Hayhurst is reprinted courtesy of *BLOOM*,
a magazine on parenting children with disabilities published by
Holland Bloorview Kids Rehab Hospital.

HarperCollins books may be purchased for educational, business, or
sales promotional use through our Special Markets Department.

HarperCollins Publishers Ltd
2 Bloor Street East, 20th Floor
Toronto, Ontario, Canada
M4W 1A8

www.harpercollins.ca

Library and Archives Canada Cataloguing in Publication
information is available upon request.

ISBN 978-1-44341-907-9

Printed and bound in the United States

RRD 9 8 7 6 5 4 3 2 1

To my friends,
who have encouraged me, pushed me,
and sometimes carried me as I wrote this book.

To William and Kate,
who gave me the greatest reason to be better.

CONTENTS

INTRODUCTION

To most Canadians, I'm the single sculler whose leg was torn open in a boating accident in the spring of 1992, but who then went on to win a bronze medal at the Summer Olympics. The miracle of my healing—calf muscles stripped to the bone, right ankle broken—followed by my triumph at Barcelona only ten weeks later made headlines around the globe.

When I was invited to tell my story to Canadian and international audiences, I witnessed how my honesty about my moments of fear, as well as my moments of courage, touched people. Some even wrote to tell me that I'd changed their lives by helping them connect to their own inner courage, opening new doors of possibility. I also came to realize through their stories that the motivational techniques I had used to fuel my physical recovery—setting goals, visualizing desired results, transforming dreams into reality—worked equally well for various mental and emotional challenges. This was incredibly rewarding. I became passionate about inspiring others, and that became my new calling.

After one keynote speech in Toronto, a woman kept pressing me. "But what made you so determined? Why did you push yourself beyond reason in Barcelona? Why didn't you give up with everything stacked against you?" Her questions reverberated inside me. I began to realize I was assuring others that they could survive anything, that they were infinitely powerful, while holding back answers that were far deeper than I was comfortable sharing. I was also experiencing periods of fury and of self-loathing that made me feel increasingly inauthentic as a motivational speaker. I knew that some truth I had spent a lifetime refusing to acknowledge was beginning to surface. I knew that I was no longer telling my whole story.

When I realized these unresolved emotions were hurting my children—the two people I loved most in the world—I decided to enter therapy. Gradually, I came to understand that recovering from my accident and winning three Olympic medals owed as much to surviving a difficult childhood as to my tough Olympic training. I also learned that I could not live fully in the present until I had taken a clear-eyed journey into my past.

In 2008, after almost seven years of living on my own, I met David Patchell-Evans, the founder of GoodLife Fitness, with whom I fell madly and deeply in love. The story of how we managed to overcome upheavals to blend our two families, including four children and assorted pets, into one "big life" rivals the dramas you might see on reality TV. Patch's profoundly autistic teenaged daughter, Kilee, taught me to reach down into reserves of patience I never knew I possessed. Though her tantrums could sometimes reduce me to screams, her unselfconscious joy could make my heart sing.

My life is good as it is, so why do I need to write a book that reveals so much of myself, and that could hurt or offend those I love? Why do I have to tear down the heroic public figure that has served me so well for so long? I gave myself every excuse for avoiding this book, but eventually I came to a place where *not* writing it became a bigger obstacle than writing it. The story raged inside me. I needed to let it out so I could face myself—my authentic self—with the acknowledgment: *Yes, this is who I am.*

I also felt that I owed the whole truth to the many people who have followed my dual careers because they believed in me. How could I explain my seemingly bulletproof character without going deeper into the messy, miserable bits that still hurt and confuse me, but that inform whatever wisdom I possess? How could I help others find their inner courage while holding back the real story of the self-doubt that continued to plague me?

People are drawn to truth. When I speak from a place of authenticity, my audience hears me: *This I know.* Sometimes they hear things I haven't even said, which is one of the remarkable gifts of public speaking: *This I also know.* People will tell you what you aren't yet sufficiently empowered to say. They feel the direction you want to go. They pick up on your facial expressions and those telltale signs of emotion that speak louder than words. They find you out.

Even though I'm terrified to be so open about my journey, I have a deep faith in people's ability to hear with their hearts. I also believe that life is a beautiful, challenging, terrible and exhilarating experience, in which we must strive to realize our greatest potential no matter how forbidding that path.

All of us see the world through our own lenses. My lens has changed profoundly over the past ten years, so that everything now looks different to me. I now see how vulnerable we all are. And how interconnected.

That's why I wish to share my story . . .

Part I

OLYMPIC MAGIC

THE ACCIDENT

Everything seemed to go wrong for me at the 1992 Rowing World Cup race in Essen, Germany.

I had arrived in this industrial city on May 11, in dismal weather, already feeling stressed. I had lost six days of training to serve as maid of honour at my sister's wedding in North Bay—an experience I wouldn't have missed for the world, but one that meant I now had to struggle to catch up to the other rowers.

The rest of the Canadian team had been in Essen for three days already, adjusting to the time change and fine-tuning their boats. I was still feeling dragged out by the flight from Toronto when I discovered my racing shell had not yet arrived. I had to use a different type of boat—an Empacher—and it felt terrible. My Swiss Stämpfli was handcrafted of wood and customized for my weight, and it sat closer to the water. The Empacher had a deeper hull, making it tippier and adding tension to the recovery of each stroke. When moving forward with the oars off the water, I count on finding a millisecond of physical recovery, but now, as my oars dove again and again without that rest, I became increasingly anxious and exhausted.

My Stämpfli finally arrived by truck from Switzerland on May 13, three days before my first race. Very few wooden boats were left in the field of international rowing, and my beautiful Stämpfli was a piece of art as well as a racing shell. I was emotionally attached to it, like a rider to a favourite mount. Sometimes, when alone in the quiet moments after a big race, I would run my hands down its smooth and slippery hull, secretly thanking it for being so good to me.

Any feeling of gratitude I had began to evaporate on May 16, the morning of my race. The sky was heavily overcast, and everything at the regatta site seemed disorganized. Though this was just a heat, with the finals to be run in the afternoon, it was still important. The World Cup was my last race before the August Olympic Games in Barcelona, and a qualifier for the Canadian Olympic team. Since I was already World Champion, I didn't fear elimination. But I still needed to prove to the Canadian Olympic Committee that I met its criteria, and finishing in the top four would signal I was in winning form.

I'd had an outstanding winter of training and was in the best shape of my life, but I was definitely feeling the pressure of being the front-runner. As the World Champion, I would not be catching anybody by surprise. I was the competitor for whom everybody else was gunning.

When I arrived at the course, I found my coach, Mike Spracklen, tightening the top nuts on the metal riggers, which hold the oarlocks, which in turn hold the oars. Once he'd finished this routine pre-race checkup, we sat down together on a bench, which was when he told me that my race format would be different from the usual. It would be a roll call.

A roll call? What was he talking about? In international regattas, heats are normally drawn the night before or on the morning of the competition, then posted on the regatta board. Roll calls were something I hadn't experienced since middle-school track meets, and certainly never in international racing. This meant I would not have an exact starting time. My race might be at 10:06 a.m. or 10:11 or 10:18. Given my high levels of adrenaline, this was unnerving. There's tremendous precision in getting a warm-up right, and the uncertainties of the roll call made this precision impossible. I needed forty minutes, but I didn't want an hour. I was always tightly strung around race time, and now I felt frustrated by the thoughtlessness of the organizers in adding this unnecessary stress. I could see no scrap of logic in it, but I knew all the other athletes were experiencing the same irritation, so I tried to remain focused on my race.

As I approached the starting gates I saw boats everywhere. Since all nineteen women in my race had to stay within earshot to learn when our heat would take place, we were rowing our shells in tight circles around the starting gates. Given that each shell was twenty-six feet long and twenty-three feet across including the oars, I couldn't take ten strokes without having to pull hard on one side to stay clear of other boats. The participants for the men's pair event preceding ours were also part of the melee. To make matters a lot worse, I could see no buoys marking off a warm-up area or indicating in which direction we should row. This was unbelievable—to not have directional buoys was unheard of.

It was a free-for-all.

Because I figured I still had time for a partial warm-up, I moved from behind the starting gates, away from the course, to where it seemed less chaotic. Without a chance to practise a few power strokes at and above race pace, my body wouldn't be ready to charge out of the gates at a stroke rate greater than forty a minute.

When I looked around, I saw no one ahead of me and only a small Laser sailboat off in the distance. I took a few deep breaths, then began my power twenty, sharp and strong, feeling the blood flow into my muscles, preparing my body for the race ahead. I had taken twelve strokes, aggressively and fluidly, when I heard a whirr like a strong wind blowing across my riggers, followed by a slight delay as my mind grasped its meaning. The German men's pair came crashing into the side of my Stämpfli with a crushing sound, fierce and screeching and devastatingly violent. I heard a man scream, low and full, and looked to see if either of the Germans was injured.

Colin von Ettingshausen's face was white and his eyes wide as he stared at my right leg. I hadn't thought to check myself for injury, but now I stared, too: it was torn open, the bone exposed and the flesh folded down so that it dangled below my ankle like a piece of meat. Flesh, bone, blood, all mangled together—it seemed unrecognizable as my leg.

This is very bad, I thought, feeling strangely calm, as if everything had slowed down. *What if my boat sinks and I drown?* I didn't want to fall into the water; in that shocked state, I was worried a shredded part of my leg would disconnect and float away.

As the shock got worse, my field of vision narrowed. I could no longer see Colin, but I could see and hear Peter

Hoeltzenbein, the other German rower, shouting for help and wildly waving his arms. He caught the attention of a safety boat. Then I started to panic. *Am I going to lose part of my leg? Can I bleed to death?*

The safety boat seemed to take forever to arrive. When it did, we saw that the driver was just a teenager. Peter assumed command, instructing the frightened youth on how to approach the two intertwined boats and how to get me into the safety boat. I ended up in Peter's arms, saying over and over, "I'm going to be all right, aren't I? Tell me I'm going to be all right."

My words were more of a command than a question.

The ride to the dock took only minutes, but it felt like hours. When I saw the German women's quad moving toward the starting gates, I fleetingly felt consumed with jealousy. *Why am I in this damned safety boat?* I wanted to be on the water prepping for my race.

A crowd had gathered on the dock. Gord Henry, our team manager, met us at the water's edge, a look of horror coming to his face when he saw my leg. He shouted to those in the volunteer ambulance to move me into their vehicle while we waited for a hospital ambulance.

Suddenly, everything seemed to speed up.

A trauma surgeon, who was a former German rower, gave me a shot of something that took the edge off the pain now searing through my leg. I was transferred to an ambulance from Essen and driven to the university hospital, where doctors applied an air cast to my lower leg. I remember joking with them in German, "Will all that air make me weigh less?" Apparently, the painkiller had allowed my German heritage to resurface, along with my humour.

Mike arrived at the hospital just as I was being wheeled back into an ambulance to be driven to a trauma centre. He looked utterly devastated. So did my boyfriend, John Wallace, a fellow rower. He accompanied me to the trauma centre, where I was examined by Dr. Friedrich Neudeck, a prominent trauma surgeon, who'd been pulled away from a World Cup soccer game. He told me that my injury required immediate surgery. The anesthesiologist, who gave me an epidural, remarked that because of my leg's muscle mass, I needed the same injection as a 200-pound man.

I was still alert enough to be proud of that.

I remember quite a lot about the start of the operation, with the doctors speaking in German and a screen preventing me from seeing what they were doing. Toward the end, a terrible shivering overcame me and I lost consciousness.

When I awoke, I was in a hospital room with John and Dr. Janice Mason, our team massage therapist. My leg was suspended above my bed, with one long screw sticking out of my foot, another sticking out of my shin, and each attached to either end of a metal bar. This, I discovered, was a Hopman's brace. I was rather pissed off that they'd drilled holes into perfectly good bones. *Don't I have enough damage without that?*

Dr. Neudeck told me that the operation had gone well, but that the extensive injury posed a significant risk of infection. During the crash, hundreds of splinters from my shattered wooden splashboard had been driven into my calf muscle, shredding away the skin. The medical team had removed as many splinters as it could; Dr. Neudeck predicted that a significant portion of the muscle would die, having been cut off from the blood supply for so long, but he assured me that the medical team had kept as much muscle on my leg as they could in hopes that I might have a slight chance of saving it.

Amidst all the ongoing trauma, I again became strangely calm. I knew everything was going to be okay. I had such a powerful connection to my body that I believed it would not fail me. Each day in training I had asked it to do the impossible, to push at crazy heart rates for hours at a time, to ignore blisters and tightening lungs and muscles heavy with lactate. Now, in the hospital room, I asked my body to heal, to keep pushing its boundaries, to figure out how to work through this injury. Despite the dire diagnosis, I persisted in seeing the accident as a slight, albeit dramatic, detour on my journey to the Barcelona Olympics.

Throughout it all, I felt supported by a positive energy— some sort of loving universal power surrounded me, and I was held. My whole being had become very still, and below that stillness was this knowingness, this conviction that I would heal. I reminded myself over and over again: I was going to be okay.

At the same time, I was aware of how serious my injury was. Each day my caregivers wondered if I would lose more muscle, which would make my leg less functional in the long term. I was in pain, and Dr. Neudeck told me that I would always walk with a limp. Since I couldn't even imagine such a possibility, I discredited his comment immediately. *Dr. Neudeck doesn't know me; he doesn't know how strong my body is!*

Whenever Janice Mason was present, her gentle spirit, always so calm and positive, filled the room. John came to the hospital every day, comforting me with his presence and providing me with anything I needed. He also went into problem-solving mode, talking to members of my family and also the reporters who had begun calling within hours of the accident. He spoke to Rowing Canada Aviron, the sport's governing body, and Sport Canada, the two organizations that were jointly paying for my treatment and recovery through their insurance. Somehow, amidst all this care and chaos, John managed to win silver with the men's eight at the Essen Regatta.

My dad, Hans, arrived on the third day of my hospital stay, very emotional, very concerned and eager to help. While happy to see him, I remained stubbornly unsentimental about how bad my injury was, focused as I was only on my healing so that I could row at the Olympics.

⋆   ⋆   ⋆

After the first few terrible days following my accident, the prognosis seemed to shift in my favour. Dr. Neudeck was startled that so much of my muscle still had integrity. I was pleased, but I wasn't incredulous like the others. I'd never entertained the idea of my muscle dying off.

The scientific explanation credited my peak condition. During the hours and hours of training with my heart rate at between 160 and 185, I had pumped so much oxygen and blood into my tissues that they possessed far greater capillarization than did the tissues of a regularly fit person. Therefore, although the accident had severed my calf muscle's main arterial blood supply, I had developed additional capillaries running up from the bottom of the cut muscle. Since these had not been damaged in the accident, they had maintained sufficient oxygenated blood for most of the muscle flap. If I had been a smoker, I would have lost all the muscle in my lower leg. Instead, over those first five days, the doctors had to shave away only tiny bits of dead tissue. They did this during two more trips to the operating room, where they also put my shattered ankle into a protective metal cage.

I was deeply grateful that my body wasn't letting me down. Here I was, lying in this hospital bed, unable to row or to run or to walk, but the cells of my body were still behaving like those of an athlete.

Meanwhile, all the calls to John's cellphone and the hospital were becoming unmanageable. For the person at the centre of this kind of crisis, the whole world weirdly shuts off. You lose your sense of time, and everything that used to matter— *What is happening to my teammates? How are Canadians reacting to my injury?*—just fades away. I didn't dare shift my focus from my healing. Every time people told me where they'd been when they'd heard about the awful accident, and how sick it had made them feel, I had to cut them off before their pessimism drained me.

Friends as well as members of Rowing Canada and the media suggested I sue the German rowers and the race organizers, but I wanted no part of it. I knew my injury would be expensive, probably requiring lifelong physiotherapy, but I also knew that the negativity involved in fighting for compensation would only hamper my healing.

I received some of the best advice from my boat builder, Melchior Burgin, who telephoned me from his home in Switzerland. Melch urged me to imagine blood pumping into my damaged muscle, and to visualize my body as strong and healthy. Although I'd been focusing on the positive, his words sounded odd—they suggested that I could do more than just believe I'd be okay, that I could actually make it so. I was unsure, but he was so adamant that I followed his advice.

Awkwardly at first, I closed my eyes, then thanked my body for being so good to me. I imagined blood surging from my heart into my muscles. I imagined the break in my ankle bone closing. Most of all, I saw myself as healed and strong. I did this every day, and one crazy thing became increasingly clear: I wasn't wanting to heal my leg just to be healthy again. I intended to row and win a medal in Barcelona, despite my lower leg being a huge open wound, with dead tissue still to be removed to decrease the risk of infection, and with a skin graft yet to come.

Even now, I marvel that I had the audacity to believe that was possible. But I did. Training for this goal had embedded itself in my soul and in my body at a cellular level, so that letting go of this dream was much harder and more painful than believing in it. To accept that my greatest hope was to walk with only a slight limp and to watch the Olympics on television was too dreadful to comprehend, so I took the easy way out of this terrible situation. I marched forward with my Olympic dream as if nothing had happened. Even in those first few days, when I felt so sick and everything was uncertain, I kept thinking of myself as an athlete in training. When other rowers consoled me about my lost Olympic dream, I was so grateful for and surprised by their attention, but I thought they were overreacting. In my mind, I was still going to the Olympics.

Just three days after my accident, I tied two stretchy Thera-Bands to the end of my bed and began to pull on them as if they were oars. I had been going crazy just lying there, hour after hour, but now, sitting upright and working my upper body, I could tap into some adrenaline and serotonin. I was certainly a hospital oddity, with my wound still open, screws driven through my foot and shin, doing a full sweaty workout on a glorified pair of bungee cords!

Every morning upon waking and every evening before falling asleep, I visualized healing. Sleep was the hardest part. Lying on my back with my leg suspended prevented me from rolling over onto my side, my default sleeping position. Often the numbness in my foot or the dull pain from the pounding of the blood streaming into my injured leg would awaken me.

I didn't like taking painkillers because they made me groggy, upset my stomach and killed my appetite. More importantly, they distracted me from experiencing the reality of my physical situation. I much preferred to breathe through the pain in an attempt to restore normalcy. When a nurse suggested my body needed rest rather than training and physiotherapy, I brushed her off. That sort of advice was for people who were sick—something for which I didn't have time. I became a bit like a bull in a china shop, barrelling over anyone or anything that got in the way of my healing. Though I tried to do this with some kindness and respect for others, I imagine my laser focus and extreme intensity left a trail of hurt. Every day meant I was one day closer to the Olympic opening ceremonies. An additional, say, three days in recovery could well mean the difference between competing or not.

Before the accident, I had often been consumed by a sense of urgency, but now my circumstances were so extreme, I knew that I would have no second chance. The deadline was real and failure too awful to imagine.

Richard Backus, our team doctor, gave some medical credence to my far-fetched intention when he arrived from Canada five days after my accident. Richard was also a dreamer who thought I might be able to work around my injury, aided by special equipment. He even drew a timeline on a napkin, indicating step by step where he felt I could be each week in my healing and retraining. In rowing, the calves aren't the powerhouse; the upper leg muscles are. If the injured portion of my lower leg could handle the force pushing through it, he felt I had a chance of competing. For this, he wanted me on Canadian soil, where I could bene-fit from the expertise and advocacy of friends. Reasonably enough, my German doctors didn't want to release me until I was stable enough to fly without too much risk of infec-tion. That meant a total of ten days in Germany. When the rest of the Canadian rowing team flew home to train for the Olympics, John stayed by my side, offering constant support. With the help of the Canadian Alpine Ski Team, which was experienced in flying injured competitors, Dr. Backus, John and a small dedicated group flew me home. We started on May 26 with an Air Canada flight to Vancouver, followed by a helicopter lift to Victoria, then an ambulance ride to Royal Jubilee Hospital.

It wasn't until I was home in Victoria, being driven in an ambulance through familiar streets, that reality over-whelmed me. The heaviness of what had happened settled down upon me and I started to cry—one of the few times since my accident.

At Royal Jubilee I was greeted by my long-time friends Marilyn and Peter Copland. Marilyn, who's all spunk and optimism, was already scheming about how to make my hospital stay fun and healthy. The homemade bread and fresh fruit she brought helped compensate for the antiquity of the hospital and my tiny room, the only private one available. We had a good laugh when we realized it had been a broom closet. It was right next to the nursing station, and the staff had cleared it of cleaning supplies so they could keep a close eye on me. Being a world-class athlete had never seemed more glamorous.

★ ★ ★

My days at Royal Jubilee were among the most intense of my life. Every morning, Marilyn arrived at seven with a homemade breakfast and a plan for the day. Dr. Backus had arranged for me to attend the outpatient physiotherapy centre, only a few feet from the hospital. Crazily enough, I was supposed to go by ambulance because I was an in-patient. Marilyn and I would wait until the nursing station was quiet, then wheel like madwomen down the hall to the elevators, giggling hysterically at our escape. Years before, when Marilyn had been stricken with cancer, I'd given her my optimism and love, and now she was repaying me tenfold. Marilyn was the best possible person with whom to share my recovery. We laughed our way through so many mishaps and ridiculous situations, and I treasured having her by my side.

John and the rest of the Canadian rowing team were now in Kamloops, 330 kilometres northeast of Victoria. They needed heat training for the temperatures they were likely to encounter at the August Olympics in Barcelona, and Kamloops was suitably hot and humid that summer. Each weekend after Saturday's practice, John drove some five hours to Victoria to spend the evening and part of Sunday with me, before driving back to Kamloops. During the week, I spoke to him every evening on the phone until I drifted off to sleep, usually around 8:30. He was an amazingly loyal partner, connecting me to my rowing buddies by relaying messages, telling me who had gone fastest in small-boat training and recounting what Mike had said that day about the eight.

Two years earlier, John and I had shown up at Mike's first Canadian training camp, after I had asked Mike to let me train along with the men. Now I felt as if I were still training with them.

* * *

As the days passed, I discovered that my physical vulnerability made me much more open and emotional with friends who came to visit. We cried together, talked about our dreams, hugged each other and said how much we loved each other. It was as if this terrible accident had opened up a special space for others to share with me.

My friend Cameron Harvey, whom I'd known since we were fifteen, was especially crucial to my recovery. He had a wacky sense of humour that could always put a smile on my face, and as his late mother had suffered from multiple sclerosis, he was experienced at pushing a wheelchair. Once, when I couldn't stand being in the hospital any longer, he took me out onto the front lawn, where I propelled myself out of my chair so I could lie on the ground with my bandaged leg in the air. It felt so good to experience the earth under my body and the sunshine on my face. Another time, we snuck out at dusk to an abandoned roundabout near the physiotherapy centre. After kicking me out of my wheelchair, Cam wheeled around the circle track at full speed, then dared me to beat his time. Driven by my Olympian competitiveness, I took up the challenge, eventually hitting a curb and dumping myself from my chair. My medical team would have recoiled in horror, but Cam and I just threw ourselves, laughing, onto the grass, where we stayed chatting for hours.

* * *

Apart from time spent with friends, my hospital days were jammed with doctors' visits, physiotherapy and a fourth operation to remove the Hopman's brace.

My physiotherapist, Jim Gow, was especially remarkable in his commitment. Each morning, he came to work at six in order to devote an hour to helping me exercise my uninjured left leg, hoping for a crossover effect to my damaged right leg. I also began to gingerly work my right leg with presses and curls using light weights.

My fifth and final operation was for my skin graft. Doctors used something that resembled a cheese slicer to peel back a couple of layers of skin from my upper right thigh, to be laid over my open leg wound. It frustrated me that the medical treatment required messing up a part of my body that was working perfectly well to heal another part. The pain after the grafting was intense—the graft site felt as if it were on fire. Even my thigh bandages were hot to the touch from my body's healing. That extra pain and damage felt like a big step backwards.

When the gauze finally came off my thigh, the flesh was red, raw and angry like a second-degree burn. My surgeon suggested I try standing for a few seconds to gradually return my body to the vertical position. I was eager to get on my feet but shocked at the intensity of the pain. My surgeon explained that the pain came from the massive damage to my circulation. He instructed me to stand for thirty seconds a couple of times a day, increasing to one minute and then to two. In my mind, if two was good, than three was better. He hadn't left the room before I was standing once again. Each time my leg would instantly turn bright purple, then sting and burn.

I trained as much as I could. Dr. Backus retrofitted a clunky, old stationary bike with handgrips instead of pedals so that I could recondition my cardiovascular system. It would sit on the bed and I would pull my wheelchair up close so I could reach the pedals. I would grind away on it for ninety minutes, Marilyn holding my wheelchair the entire time so it didn't rock and shake. I had an old Led Zeppelin video CD that I played over and over to help pass the time. It was great to be pumping blood through my muscles hard enough to feel that familiar athletic fatigue. I knew my body was accomplishing heroic amounts of healing—my broken ankle bone knitting, my calf muscles repairing and, of course, the large skin graft on my thigh mending. Yet despite the delicious food the Coplands brought me every day, my weight was dropping so fast that my tightest shorts hung from me. I was so desperate for calories that I drank the sugary processed apple juice every hospital seems to have until even the smell nauseated me.

I remained fiercely focused on the positive. Friends who arrived with dramatic stories about an uncle's dropped foot or a cousin's infected injury were not invited back. Harsh as my actions may have seemed, I just couldn't handle that kind of stress—as my sister, Daniele, learned the hard way. I adore Daniele, and she'd flown all the way from Halifax to be with me in Victoria. She's a busy lawyer who reviews medical files for Veterans Affairs Canada, and while I was awaiting my skin graft, she started telling me about clients whose grafts had become infected, with appalling results. She was concerned—probably rightly—that I would push myself too hard, too soon, with devastating results. She was trying to protect me, but I didn't want to hear it. I screamed, "Stop it. Just stop it! Don't say one more negative word about anything." After a short cooling-off period, Daniele was back by my side—this time with only positive stories to share.

I started to realize that quite a few of my friends saw the world through a murky lens, rather than focusing on all that is possible. We had always worked well as yin and yang—they were attracted to my optimism and strength, while I found them grounding. But now, being grounded felt like being dragged down. Since I had nothing to spare for them, I eliminated them from my life in one brutal stroke. I had a great excuse: I was focused on becoming the best in the world once again, and I had to invest everything I possessed to accomplish my crazy dream.

What I remember most about the aftermath of my accident is the many people who stopped their lives for me. My dad travelled from Toronto to Germany, and my sister from Halifax to Victoria. A small group dropped by every second day with tasty food to tempt my appetite. John visited every weekend, which must have put him in a difficult situation with the rest of the guys in the men's eight. Instead of eating and sleeping in preparation for their next five days of relentless Olympic training, he was exhausting himself to support me.

When the husband of my rowing friend Brenda Colby saw my leg—torn apart, inflamed and discoloured—he felt so faint he had to leave. Brenda not only settled in for a long, quiet conversation, but also gave my ugly swollen foot a massage.

Sometimes I fell asleep during these friendly visits because my body was working double time, trying to heal from a massive injury as well as keeping me in Olympic condition. My body may have been exhausted, but my spirit couldn't be contained. I yearned to get out on the water once again. I yearned to be rowing stroke by powerful stroke toward my dream, but the graft site posed too great a risk of infection. I was hospital-bound at Royal Jubilee for nine days.

THE RECOVERY

Two days after I was released from Royal Jubilee Hospital and twenty-three days after my accident, Peter Copland drove me to nearby Elk Lake for a row. I was still in a wheelchair. I was wearing a prosthesis on my right leg. Even standing still caused me excruciating pain.

Since my Stämpfli was in Switzerland being repaired, Jon Elmquist, the National Team boatman, and Geoffrey Hall, designer of my leg prosthesis, had adapted a wooden Hudson for me. Jon had replaced the right foot stretcher with a pivoting metal plate so that each time I moved forward to take a stroke, my right foot pivoted. This felt far less powerful than pushing off a stable platform, but it did ease pressure on my broken ankle. It was a trade-off—at least in theory.

Peter, Jon, Geoffrey and Dr. Backus wheeled me down to the dock. With the help of Dr. Backus, I managed, somewhat unceremoniously, to get into the racing shell. I leaned out to secure the oarlocks. I fiddled with the foot stretchers. Then I shoved off.

As my team waited in anticipation, I took a couple of

strokes to test the adaptations. The rotating foot stretcher felt strange, but excitement took over as soon as my blade gripped the water. My legs pushed against the foot stretchers; I pulled with my back and my arms, and the boat underneath me took off. I was flying!

My onshore team was in a panic. They hadn't yet put the safety boat in the water because they hadn't expected me to row away. By the time they realized what was happening, I was too far down the lake to hear them yell. Even if I had, I doubt I would, or could, have stopped my thrilling, energy-filled strokes. This was no time to be tentative. I had arrived in a wheelchair and couldn't stand without pain, but now I was back in my element, slicing through the water in my adapted scull on a lake whose every coastal indentation, every smell and sound, I knew and loved.

I hadn't read any newspapers or watched television in the hospital, so I wasn't fully aware of how the entire country had been following my recovery. Those around me knew what a national story I had become and were far more tuned in to other people's investment in my recovery than I was. Now they were paranoid that something might happen to me, especially with so many water skiers zipping across Elk Lake, creating wakes all around me. This was a risk I wasn't prepared to see in my sheer joy at being on the water. I put myself through the fullest workout I could, pushing myself to exhaustion. I was eager to squeeze through that narrow window of opportunity in order to be fit enough and fast enough to compete at Barcelona.

Back on shore, I remained totally reliant on others to drive, to cook, to do my laundry and to help change my bandages.

Marilyn and Peter Copland had offered to be my caregivers for as many weeks as necessary, and so I moved into Home Bay, their place on an acre of waterfront on Cordova Bay, with its spectacular gardens. Jon and Geoffrey installed my rowing machine on the Coplands' deck, where I could enjoy the sound of the ocean. Like my boat, it had been adapted so that one foot rotated at the catch of the stroke, reducing the stress on my damaged ankle. Using it felt awkward, yet it was much closer to rowing than cranking on a Monarch stationary bike, as I had in the hospital.

Of course, I could hardly wait to return to Elk Lake, where I worked out every day, sometimes with Cam, who took a week's vacation from work to train beside me. Because water skiers were not restricted at that time, they shot all over the place, creating waves. When they came too close, I would verbally challenge them, the adrenaline coursing through my body. On one occasion, I cursed with such menace at a boat driver who'd cut me of that Peter intervened before the conflict could get out of hand. He was so diplomatic in explaining my situation that the boat driver became extremely apologetic. All I could think of was how little time I had to get back in form. Having to row in the wakes of pleasure vehicles made me furious.

After three days, I did my first timed test. I had lost a lot of conditioning while lying in a hospital bed, and the adapted foot stretcher caused me to push less forcefully with my right leg, making my stroke uneven and reducing my power. I was rowing slowly, and I knew it. A 2,000-metre race that used to take me 7 minutes and 25 to 30 seconds now took 8 minutes and 43 seconds. My hopes were dashed. One minute and

15 seconds seemed like an impossible gap to make up in six weeks, when just half a second could mean the difference between a medal and a fourth-place defeat.

I returned to the Coplands' saddened and discouraged, but something shifted inside me that night. I let go. I let go of controlling, measuring and judging the progress of my recovery. That wouldn't work, and I knew it. Instead, I fell into the wonder of everything that was happening by opening myself up to potential miracles. That was the approach I'd taken those first days in the hospital, and it was the path I still needed to follow. I wasn't going to time myself anymore. I was going to focus on my day-to-day improvement, celebrating that I could stand for a couple of minutes at a time, that I could row for an hour at a time, that my rowing technique was slowly adapting and returning.

Once again, this positive approach transformed my training into something tremendously exciting. Because I had so far to go, I could now experience myself advancing in leaps and bounds. Usually at this stage in my Olympic training, I'd be measuring improvement by a fraction of a second, by slight changes to the feel of the boat, by tiny physical and mental advances. Recovering from my injury had temporarily turned me into a novice. Each time I rowed, the boat would feel more comfortable, a chunk of my conditioning would return and I would tap into a huge amount of muscle memory. But it was more than muscle memory. Some mornings, upon opening my eyes, I felt as if I were entering a fantastical land. If someone had told me that to reach the starting gates in Barcelona I'd have to walk on my hands, I would have tried to do it, while believing that I could. Some evenings, in those brief moments before entering a deep and exhausted sleep, I felt utterly in awe of the process unfolding in my life.

It wasn't always magical. One day, while hopping around the Copland house, I tripped on my laundry and fell squarely on my damaged leg. The pain was bad enough, but the fear that I'd set myself back was worse. Just to look at my leg was still shocking. The damage was so horrifically visible, with steel through my leg, a raw open wound and an ugly graft with angry skin. My reality right then and the dream of being at the Olympics in only a few weeks, competing with the strongest and toughest rowers in the world, was a pretty big disconnect. At times, I felt I'd go insane from the numbness in my foot, from the terrible throbbing in my damaged leg. It took all my skill at breath control and distraction to get me through the night. Nevertheless, the rest of my body felt phenomenally healthy, and I retained a positive relationship with my injured leg. It had taken on its own identity, and I would talk to it, asking it to do more than it was ready to do.

Also offsetting my appalling reality was the dream that for a decade had been earning an increasingly concrete and legitimate place in my life. In 1984, when I was only nineteen, I had won an Olympic bronze medal in double sculls with my sister, Daniele. In the 1985 World Championships, I had finished fourth in single sculls. In 1990, I had won silver, and in 1991, I had won gold. Now, at age twenty-seven, becoming an Olympic Champion in single sculls would be the fulfillment of my dream. I couldn't just let that go. My calf muscles might be shredded and my ankle broken, but I couldn't stop visualizing myself competing with the athletes with whom

I'd already shared the world stage. That was where I belonged, not sidelined as a spectator.

I remained ruthless about keeping my environment optimistic by barring all negativity. I also avoided long-term thinking about my leg or the hideous scar the accident and surgery would leave. I refused to indulge in thoughts of *Why me, why now, when I'm poised to realize a lifetime dream of winning Olympic gold?* I was grateful not to have lost my leg. I was grateful not to have become paralyzed. I was grateful that the German boat had not collided into mine a fraction of a second later, searing through my kidneys and other internal organs. All this gave me a huge feeling of peace, allowing me to drop all worry and to just go for it.

A week after I was released from the hospital, my agents, Elliott Kerr and Andrea Shaw, wheeled me to the door of a reception room in the Empress Hotel for my first public appearance since the accident. The room was filled with journalists, many of whom I knew but more of whom I didn't. Flashbulbs exploded continuously as I wheeled up to the podium, where twenty microphones awaited me. That's when it dawned on me how intensely Canadians had been following my story.

It was a little intimidating, but I've always been comfortable with the press, and I was happy to report on how well I was doing after weeks of isolation. I tried just to be myself, answering questions honestly and simply. Of course, the big one was "Are you going to the Olympics?" It felt good not to have to own this question but simply to say that I was doing my best, just living each moment of this crazy, challenging and, yes, at times wonderful experience.

The whole media event felt both touching and overwhelming. When I had first voiced my intention to compete in the Olympics, those closest to me were probably just indulging my fantasies to help me cope with my ghastly injury. Their minds opened a little when Dr. Backus supported the idea by drawing his graph indicating the steps I could take in my retraining. John already knew the force of my determination and in about the third or fourth week of my recovery accepted my view as no longer outrageous, and even spent part of each weekend in my coach boat helping me train. Several times he told me over the phone how much I was inspiring him and his teammates. Mike Rascher, one of the men's eight, wrote me a beautiful note recounting how the team had loaded my old blue boat on the trailer going to Kamloops as a sign that I was with them in spirit. I read that note over and over, imagining my boat at the training camp and knowing that the guys expected me to return.

I didn't at first know what Coach Mike Spracklen thought about my Olympic chances. He and I were so spiritually and emotionally close that he himself seemed traumatized by my trauma. I didn't understand that reaction until years later when I had children. That's when I realized that while I might be practical and fairly nonchalant about wounds to myself, any cuts to my children requiring stitches would catapult me into extremes of grief and anxiety. On June 30, when I showed up at Mike's pre-Olympic training camp in Aiguebelette, France, all my concerns dissolved. Now back in his element, Mike knew exactly what to do, which meant treating me like any other competitor. I wasn't sick or ailing. I was an athlete in the final stages of Olympic preparation. We agreed that we would push as hard as we could every day unless I told him that it was too much. We both knew this was my only chance of regaining the fitness and agility I had lost.

I completely trusted Mike. He was selfless in his desire to do everything he could to help his athletes. Each day, after spending two hours coaching the men, he coached me. As always, he made sure that my boat was fitted to my specific needs, checking the pitch of the oarlocks and the wear on the oar sleeves. He also insulated me from the media and handled communications with the Canadian Olympic Association and Rowing Canada so that I could focus on my training and on becoming faster.

Mike had made it clear that my wheelchair was not an option at training camp. Boarding the plane on my way to France was the last time I used it, and good riddance! Since I found it tiring to walk farther than a few hundred feet with my cane, the team rented a car so that John or Mike could drive me the short distance to the course each morning.

I was making progress where it really counted. My boat was no longer adapted; the pivoting metal plate had been removed and the foot stretcher reinserted, as I needed the firmness and increased power of a stable platform. The first time I tried rowing, the painful tension on my broken ankle was extreme, but within days I had adjusted by blocking the constant throbbing and the swelling from consciousness, focusing instead on working through the familiar pain of training.

We pushed fast and hard those four weeks in France. I'd initially felt let down by Mike's reaction to my accident because I'd wanted him to be more present, more resolute. Now, with Mike in coaching mode, I found myself uplifted by his belief that I was going to the Olympics as a serious contender, not as a consolation prize for the hard work I'd put into my recovery.

My rowing buddies in the men's eight also provided a positive backdrop to my inner journey. They were inspiring to watch on the water, their strokes so crisp and so powerful and so synchronized. I felt overwhelmed with excitement about how much they were achieving, how far they'd come and the thrill of the dream we shared. We'd all taken this journey together to become the best in the world, and while I wasn't rowing in the same boat, I definitely felt I'd earned their respect. Since March 1990, when John and I had shown up at Mike's first Canadian training camp, we had all performed the workouts together, cried through the tough days, pushed each other for more repetitions on the weights and competed for a faster run. I'd also put up with their guy talk, their farting and burping, their mid-workout cussing—albeit with some self-censoring, as I obviously wasn't one of the guys. I respected each of them deeply, and I wanted them to realize their dream of Olympic gold. After their silver win at the 1991 World Championships in Vienna, I knew only gold would seem like a victory to them.

These men had also been greatly impacted by my injury, but that didn't stop them from stealing my cane to imitate the way I walked. They were also curious about my scar. Don Telfer of the men's four, with whom I had a special friendship, was the first to ask to see my leg. When he did, he just shook his head in amazement. Andy Crosby, a madcap who's unique, smart and funny, was next in line. His reaction was "Holy shit!"

When word spread about how dramatic my wound was, the other guys found their way into physio one by one so they could be both thrilled and horrified. By then, the media was describing my presence in training camp with expressions of awe, so this sharing of delicious grossness with the guys brought me, in their eyes, back down to their level in some way. And my injury *was* gross. Because the graft skin from my thigh hadn't stretched all the way across my leg wound, part was still open and seeping.

As well as the horror show, the guys and I shared a lot of humour. I suppose the sheer volume and intensity of the training made us a little punch-drunk, so that we found the silliest things hilarious. After each meal, when the stinky-sock cheese plate came around, we would all laugh, offending the French chef, who considered cheese next to God. We would dare each other to try the hard cheese with the mould growing in it—the piece that had been sitting on the plate for days. Later, we all snacked on bread and chocolate in our rooms.

Despite our hijinks, pressure was mounting on the men's eight. In our first week of training, the team wasn't jelling as Mike had wanted, and the rowers were becoming edgy and a little insecure. That's when Mike made a startling decision: he removed John from the prestigious stroke seat, shuffling the team so John would be in the bow and Derek Porter would be in stroke. The stroke sets the rhythm and decides with the coxswain, calling the race from the front of the boat, when to vary the rate. John had held the stroke seat for three years, so losing it was a huge blow. I knew he was hurting, and I couldn't help but feel that the time he'd spent helping me to recover had factored into Mike's decision. By staying at my bedside in Germany, John had missed ten days' training at Kamloops. Then, by commuting each weekend to Royal Jubilee Hospital, he'd probably further strained his relationship with the rest of the team.

I was upset that John had been knocked back, and the fact that it was only five weeks before Barcelona made it extra stressful. With demonstrable class, he accepted Mike's decision, then threw himself into supporting Derek and adapting to the bow, where everything moves just that fraction of a second faster. Since John didn't seem crushed, or at least didn't let on to me how he felt, I figured it was best to take my lead from him and to keep moving forward. As he said, "I would rather win gold in bow seat than lose gold in stroke."

* * *

Those weeks in that tiny French village held a special kind of enchantment. With my regular life stripped away, it was just me, the men I'd grown to love and the workouts. Every day mattered, and to spend each one surrounded by spectacular scenery, under sunny skies that radiated over the pristine lake, added to the splendour of this time when everything seemed possible.

Still walking with a cane, I would get on the lake in early evening, after the men's eight had finished training. The water would be quiet and flat, and I'd do a full workout. Over and over, I sculled down the course, with Mike asking for a little more crispness on the technical side, a little more push with my legs, a little more relaxation through the shoulders.

Sometimes he would exclaim in wonder, "You're going as fast as before your accident!"

On the tenth day, with John also in the coach boat, we started our afternoon practice late to avoid some of the heat. Mike had set up this workout, consisting of twenty one-minute repeats with the focus on speed. That meant I would row as hard and as fast as I could for one minute, then rest for one minute, then repeat this sequence, again and again.

We finished the first set of ten, then moved on to the second. Mike was full of encouragement and praise—"Well done, Silken!" Though it was growing dark by the time we finished the second set, he asked if I wanted to do five more. I was game for anything that would move me a little closer to winning a medal in Barcelona.

Now, after each minute, Mike just shook his head, then began discussing how fast I was going with John. I was too focused to hear, and it wasn't until later, after the workout, that he shared my times with me. *How could this be? How could I, with a bandaged leg, a broken ankle and massive skin damage, row twenty-five consecutive one-minute sprint pieces at race pace?*

John was just as incredulous. No matter how hard I did a piece, I would go as fast the next time and the next. None of us could put what was happening into words, but we were all moved and full of wonder. When I clocked better than before my accident, Mike exclaimed in disbelief, "This is amazing."

At age twenty-seven, I still lived strongly in the concrete and the rational, but the intensity of this time allowed me to put that attitude aside long enough to acknowledge that other mysterious forces were at play. Recovering from such a severe injury in so short a time defied probability. Something special had taken over, something that everyone close to me who was at all open to the unusual could feel. It was as if I were being carried along in a fabulous dream where extraordinary events were part of the norm. All of us knew we were witnessing a little miracle, and no one wanted to disrupt its rhythm by talking too much about it.

Knowing that something surreal was at play on some sub-conscious level allowed me to relax into the miracle of it all. I didn't even feel as if I were using every single molecule to force myself through pain back to health. Instead, I felt I was opening myself to a process that was carrying me along. It was a huge relief to know I wasn't alone in this Mount Everest of a journey—that greater forces were propelling me so that one day soon I would stand on the Olympic podium.

THE RACE

On July 19, the Canadian rowing team and I arrived in Spain for the Olympics, then settled into our accommodations about 125 kilometres outside Barcelona. One of the great perks of being rowers was that during the Olympics, we lived in a satellite village on the water rather than downtown. Our location on breathtakingly beautiful Lake Banyoles was far easier for me to navigate with my cane, my prosthesis and my newly grafted wound than chaotic Barcelona, where the vast majority of the sporting competitions were being held.

Banyoles provided another advantage: since journalists had to travel ninety minutes to get to our venue, they were less likely to arrive unannounced. We *did* have media. Every other day, I held a press conference to state how my leg was healing, how my body was adjusting to the heat and what my expectations were for the upcoming competition. Even though I didn't have much that was newsy to report, holding these conferences allowed me to focus on my training without having to worry about being ambushed.

I like journalists. I had once worked with them as a

publicist for Penguin Books, which was my first job out of college. Most who covered our sport were respectful, with some proving to be special people for whom I had a lot of time. But in France I had been set upon by an NBC-TV crew that arrived unannounced, then rented a boat to follow me around the lake. It was quite a frightening experience—my own minor version of being chased by the paparazzi, which I was relieved to find wasn't an issue in Spain.

In the days before any important race, I typically suffer attacks of fear and self-doubt. *Why did I become a single sculler? Why am I putting myself through so much solitary pressure?* These thoughts were always intertwined with much older and more complex feelings about not being a good enough person, about not deserving to compete at this level, about the dread that I would choke.

Three days before my first race in Spain, I became so nervous I could barely eat. Two days before the race, fear gripped me so deeply that I started to shake while taking a shower. I stood under the streaming water, crying and shaking and trying to convince myself that I would be okay. The pressure was terrible, but it was also familiar. I knew from past experience that this stress was part of my mental preparation. I also knew it would break at the moment I couldn't stand the anxiety and terror any longer.

Some athletes play cards or socialize to relieve the pressure, but I liked to get my head into the race early, and to stay there with laser-like focus, adrenaline high. Now, each day, I played the race over and over in my mind, visualizing each fluid stroke and imagining a feeling of strength. Every night, lying in bed, I replayed it several more times, then fell asleep while visualizing numbers counting backwards from 100. Oftentimes I wished I could prepare myself differently, but I seemed to need to go through these stages to come out of the starting gates sharp and aggressive.

And, of course, the races in Barcelona were different from all others. Highlighting their specialness was that I had been asked if I would consider carrying the Canadian flag to the Opening Ceremony. This would have been an incredible thrill, yet I knew I couldn't allow anything to distract me from training and healing. Oh, how I wish I could have embraced this honour! How I wish I could have just rolled with it and made it part of my preparation, but I wasn't that kind of athlete. I was afraid that carrying the flag—indeed, even attending the Opening Ceremony—might take me over the edge of anxiety, costing me a medal.

In the midst of all this high tension, I experienced a longing to feel the softness of grass, to hear the gentle rustle of wind, to drink in the fresh air. Thirty-six hours before my first race, I lay down in the shade of a big old tree by Lake Banyoles, gathering my resources. It was late afternoon. The journalists and most of the officials had gone. In the background I could hear the occasional rower glide by and the murmur of voices as athletes and coaches exchanged their final post-practice observations.

Some of the extra stress I'd been carrying started to leak out in tears that ran down my face. *What if my body, after all it has endured, gives out on me?* All rowers have to come to terms with the knowledge that to race means hurting ourselves. With muscles screaming and lungs bursting, we must push harder still. There's no way around it. *What if I don't have the guts to row a great race? What if I find myself far behind, unable to summon the courage to hurt myself more?*

From late afternoon until early evening, I struggled to let go of these fears, looking for the courage to enter my starting gates in an aggressive, tunnel-vision mode, focused only on that medal podium directly ahead. I reminded myself of all my training. I assured myself that all the other racers were just as scared, even if they didn't show it.

At last, my anxieties peaked. I grew calmer. I let go of my mental spinning and became centred. I was no longer at the Barcelona Olympics, with hundreds of journalists awaiting my next move. I was just myself, stretched across the earth, surrounded by beauty.

*   *   *

For my first heat on July 28, I drew Anne Marden, a US rower who'd won silver in the 1988 Seoul Olympics. Considering that I hadn't competed in almost three months, I rowed a solid race, but my pacing was off and Anne beat me. I knew I had to notch up my performance to make the final, though I had been close enough to signal that I was in the game.

Between races, I spent every spare minute in physiotherapy, attempting to reduce the swelling of my leg. My physiotherapist, Brian Gastaldi, with whom I'd worked as a student at Western University, wrapped my foot and calf in an inflatable cold bag in hopes that the pressure and freezing would help my wound recover from the exertion and the heat. The daytime temperature in Barcelona was often an incredible 38°C. With the sun relentlessly beating down on my shoulders, it was a mental dance trying to decide whether to wear a T-shirt to constantly dip into the water to bring down my core temperature and avoid sunburn, or to wear a half-top to increase the exposed skin surface so my sweat could evaporate. I rotated between the two, taking my T-shirt on and off over my sports half-top to minimize the chance of heat stroke. It didn't help that I was forced to wear bandages over most of my leg—including one on my thigh to maintain pressure on the healing skin, and a stocking on my calf to improve circulation and to protect the graft from the sun. I also wore a large piece of plastic, shaped to my injured leg like Silly Putty, so that an accidental smack wouldn't gape open the wound.

I was quite a spectacle during those Olympics, leaning on my cane as I made my way through the boat area, my right leg bandaged. In the Olympic Village, I was aware of other athletes staring and whispering as I hobbled to the dining hall, but without exception, all were kind and supportive. I don't think anybody believed I could win anything, since I still had a broken ankle and was in a lot of pain.

My semifinal took place two days after I had been beaten by Anne Marden. It's a race for which every rower is tense, as twelve people are competing for six spots in the final, and one mistake makes the difference between competing for gold and realizing that the best you can place is seventh.

I had a spectacular race, rowing sharp and strong. I shocked myself, as well as the rest of the field, when I came in first. That's when my competitors shifted from cheering me on as the underdog to vowing to beat me. Not only did that win mark me as a real contender for a medal, but it was also critical in lifting my confidence for the final, two days away. I would be entering it ranked number two on all-over performance, with Elisabeta Lipa of Romania, Annelies Bredael of Belgium and possibly Anne Marden as the rowers to beat.

My dad was so nervous the day of the semifinals that he and my stepmother, Laura, had arrived at the grandstand without their tickets, which he'd forgotten in his fluster. Earlier that summer, he'd broken his arm while trying to paint his house, and now, in his rush to get back from his rented villa with the tickets, he leapt over a ditch, fell and rebroke it. Only after I had won my race did his adrenaline sink low enough for his arm to start hurting. He would require a new cast. That evening we swam in his villa's pool—his broken arm sticking high out of the water and my leg lifted beside it.

★　★　★

The Olympic final to decide which three women single scullers were the best in the world was on August 2.

The night before any big race is always frustrating for me, because no matter how tired I am and how much I yearn for a good sleep, I'm always too stressed to mentally park the race and pretend the next day will be normal. Whereas most athletes worry about racing sleepless, I realized long ago that this would have no bearing on my performance because the adrenaline coursing through my body would be more than ample to shake off any fatigue.

As always, I struggled to nurture a mindset whereby little things didn't matter. After all my training, I refused to let winning depend on liking last night's dinner or receiving the blessing of any one person. I'd also intentionally avoided becoming superstitious, so that I wasn't going to be freaking out in a search for my favourite socks. Same with becoming too dependent on routines, because so many details are out of an athlete's control. Suddenly, weather causes a delay, or a nervous stomach makes you take longer than usual in the bathroom, or a hypervigilant official on the dock insists on very slowly checking everything in a boat for safety.

In the hours before the event, while I was still on land, my mind was racing. I repeatedly ran to the bathroom; I felt my chest tighten, and I heard the strain in my voice as I almost choked with nervousness.

Among other rowers, I'm well known for my startle reflex. At any loud noise, I jump out of my chair. If someone suddenly touches my shoulder from behind, I scream and jump. That's why I'm so great at starts—my reflexes are highly attuned for flight. I used to joke that I was "born ready," but that readiness has grown exhausting over the years.

When Mike came to give me his pep talk, I was ready to hear his tips on strategy or some insightful observation about my competitors. Instead, he held my hand, looked into my eyes and told me he loved me. That threw me. At that stage in my life, I didn't know how to handle such deep sentiments. It took a few minutes to shake off the softness his words created, and to become hard and edgy for the race ahead. Yet maybe Mike knew me better than I knew myself, because my greatest struggle as an athlete is managing the incredible amounts of adrenaline and anxiety rushing through my system.

Even before I put my boat on the water, I knew I was going to push fast through those first 1,000 metres. Then, when my lungs became sharp through lack of oxygen and my muscles screamed with lactic acid, I was going to breathe through the pain, relax, and stay alert and strong.

Because I was ranked number two, I received one of the favoured centre lanes, which meant I could more easily watch the other five racers. As I backed my boat into the starting gate for the 2,000-metre final, I was startled to see photographers from all over the world leaning against each other on my dock, poised to get a shot of this Canadian Comeback Kid. Most of my competitors had only a couple of cameras pointed at them, but my dock was almost sinking from the weight of the photographers. I smiled to myself at the silliness of it all—I didn't think of myself as a comeback story. I was just another racer hungry to win.

I checked my oarlocks—a habit begun ten years before when I saw a Romanian sculler tip out of her boat 250 metres into the race because she had failed to tighten hers.

I felt focused and calm as the starter began the roll call: "Romania, ready?

"France, ready?

"Canada, ready?"

And so on.

After each of us had given the nod, a short pause and then, "Are you ready? Go!"

The pistol cracked.

In a wild flurry, the six of us exploded out of the gates. I could hear the movement of the collars hitting the oarlocks and the whirring of the safety boats as I focused on breathing deep and strong, on pulling crisp and fast, on driving my legs down explosively.

Typically, I shot out of the gates fast and cleanly, my mind without thought, my body all instinctive reaction and muscle memory for the first 250 metres. It was usually close to a minute before I would change gears by taking my stroke rate down slightly, then switching into the rhythm I would keep through the body of the race.

This day was no different.

For that first 500 metres, thoughts of my injured leg did not enter my mind. I was rowing the way I'd been trained to row, and as I went through the 300-metre mark, I found a sweet, strong rhythm—powerful and explosive, light and fluid—that made me feel as if I could row forever. That lasted only a few seconds, till I was nearing the 500-metre mark. I was solidly in the pack, but Elisabeta Lipa, the Romanian, had already taken an enormous lead. Elisabeta is an amazing athlete. I had been competing against her since the 1984 Los Angeles Olympics, where she and her partner won gold in double sculls, while my sister and I won bronze. Then, in the 1991 World Championships, I had beaten her to win gold. Elisabeta's strategy was always to race from ahead, often gaining such a decisive lead that she was impossible to reel back. To beat Elisabeta, you had to keep within striking distance in hopes that she'd blow up, which she'd done a couple of times, most notably in the 1990 World Championships final. Just when she'd gained such a strong lead it looked like no one could catch her, she completely lost it, to finish last. That's the wonderful, terrible thing about this sport. Nobody is great all the time. We're always having to prove ourselves each race, each season.

At Banyoles, though, I wasn't worried about Elisabeta. I

was totally focused on myself, in the fight of my life. As I came through that first 500 metres, I'd had a clue that my conditioning was different from before the accident. My strokes felt less lively and more laboured, and I was struggling for oxygen—a feeling unfamiliar to me, since aerobic fitness was usually my strong suit. Those feelings passed quickly as I moved into the body of the race, finding a strong rhythm while fighting to stay connected to the front-runners. This is where the race starts to unfold. Anyone can sprint out of the gates, but keeping an aggressive tempo, a fluid rhythm and a quick pace, stroke after stroke, reveals an athlete's fitness level and how in sync she is that day. My years of training, combined with adrenaline and a racing mindset, had taken me three-quarters through, but some of my sharpness was gone.

Only 500 metres to go.

All of us raised our stroke rate in the surge to the finish line. I could feel my muscles tightening and my chest constricting. As Anne Marden, a strong finisher, once again pushed ahead of me, I realized that I might place fourth. *Fourth?* That was unbearable.

I could hear the crowd roar—crazy amounts of noise for a rowing race, amplified by the enthusiastic Canadians filling the floating grandstands. I had nothing left. I was seizing up. My head was foggy, but I was *not* going to come in fourth. At that moment, some force took hold of my oars. I lifted my rate—one, two, then three strokes more a minute. My body had been trained for this sprint, and now a force of power, love and grace drove my boat ahead of Anne's and over the finish line. I was so confused with exhaustion and my body's screaming from lactic acid, I didn't know where I'd finished. When I read the scoreboard—Gold: Romania, Lipa, Elisabeta; Silver: Belgium, Bredael, Annelies; *Bronze: Canada, Laumann, Silken*—I breathed a sigh of relief. Not elation, not a triumphant fist-in-the-air punch, just relief and exhaustion, and an amazing, encompassing feeling of completion.

I had done it.

There was a media scrum immediately after the race. When CTV's Rod Black tried to interview me, it made for a hilarious moment of reality TV. I was so exhausted that all you could hear was me huffing and puffing, trying to gasp a coherent answer, until finally I just shook my head with the impossibility of it all.

* * *

The men's eight race was only two hours after mine. The guys had cheered me on, and John was waiting at the finish line to give me a hug. Now they were having their pre-race pep talk as they prepared to get on the water. I didn't have a chance to wish them luck, but every last remnant of my energy was directed their way.

While I was ending my first round of interviews, a CTV crew member told me that Gerry Dobson and Roger Jackson wanted me to join them at the finish line to help with commentary for the men's eight. Everything in my body just wanted to stop, lie down and pass out, but, wow, what a great opportunity to share with Canada all I knew my guys would be going through. I was also grateful because I think I would have thrown up just watching the race without the discipline of having to make intelligent comments. We followed it on screen, then live as the boats came into view down the 2,000-metre course. I was very professional for the first 1,500 metres, expressing what I thought the rowers would be thinking and feeling. The Canadians led from the beginning, but with about 450 metres to go, the Romanians and Germans began to move up, cutting our lead foot by foot, inch by inch.

"Go, go, go!" I screamed, the broadcast headset still on.

At two metres to the finish, our guys were just hanging on. We won gold by fourteen-hundredths of a second.

The Canadian rowing team was elated, all our emotions running incredibly high. The women's pair had won gold, the women's eight had won gold, the women's four had won gold. I'd won a single's bronze, and now here was the men's eight with gold. I don't know whether Mike's last-minute decision to switch John from stroke had made the boat run faster, but psychologically the shuffle seemed to have re-energized the team by lifting their confidence, and the way John had handled the change endeared him even more to his teammates after they'd won.

For Canadian rowers, Barcelona 1992 was a landslide. We had accomplished everything anyone had dared expect—and more.

⋆　⋆　⋆

Apart from watching the men's eight, I don't remember too much about the hours after my race. They went by as if I were in a dream. I do remember a CTV cameraman telling me he'd never seen anyone look so exhausted. The moment the pressure came off, my body let go. I managed to stir up just enough energy to smile and thank everybody before going to my room and falling into such a deep sleep that I missed the team party and breakfast the following morning.

I have only impressions, rather than detailed memories, of the next few days, because that's how long it took for me to become human again. I know Mike Spracklen and others checked in on me, but I was totally and utterly finished, and it wasn't until our rowing team packed up from our village and headed to Barcelona that I started to have fun. I went with the German team to a party sponsored by Mercedes-Benz, dancing all evening on my good leg. Wine and my still-surging adrenaline dulled the pain, but in the morning my wounded leg was swollen and sore. Nevertheless, I had been focused and resolute for so long that I was thrilled to forget about my injury for a change, go a little crazy and stay up till 5 a.m.

One event does remain indelible in my memory: the Canadian Olympic team honoured me by selecting me to carry Canada's flag into the stadium for the August 8 Closing Ceremony. When I heard my name announced in front of my teammates, the floodgates opened and the emotion of the summer was finally released. The next day, the newspapers showed a very red-faced, puffy-eyed version of me holding the flag.

Fair enough. I'd forced myself to forgo the thrill of carrying our flag into the Opening Ceremony; now good fortune had come full circle to find me.

FAME

Despite the rush of media in Barcelona, nothing prepared me for my reception back in Canada. On August 10, I snuck into Toronto's Pearson International Airport under the radar, stayed overnight at my dad's Mississauga home, then went downtown the next day to see my agent. As I walked along Richmond Street, every person I passed—every single one!—waved or stopped me to say how much my medal had meant to them. Taxi drivers honked. One man jumped out of his cab, threw his arms around me and exclaimed, "You make me proud to be a Canadian!"

I was in shock. The story of my bronze medal had made the front page of every major paper in the country. Overnight, I'd become a household name, and of course Elliott, my agent, urged me to take advantage of every opportunity, as Olympic athletes usually have only a small window in which to build a brand.

I went into overdrive. I did photo shoots for *Chatelaine* and *Newsweek*. I was presented with the keys to Mississauga, my home town, by Mayor Hazel McCallion. I had streets in

Mississauga and Newmarket named after me. I received the first of four honorary degrees from the University of Victoria (followed by McMaster, Laurentian, the University of Windsor and Western). I inspected the guard at Toronto's Royal Agricultural Winter Fair. I was invited to a luncheon with Princess Diana in Vancouver (which I had to decline because I was in Toronto). I went with the rest of the Olympic team to visit Governor General Ray Hnatyshyn, and to the House of Commons to meet with Prime Minister Brian Mulroney.

It was a whirlwind of once-in-a-lifetime experiences: Alfred Sung offered me a whole wardrobe from his ritzy Yorkville store and the Blue Jays asked me to throw the open-ing pitch at a game. Before the pitch, Elliott, who loves base-ball, asked me if I knew how to throw. As it turned out, I didn't, so to avoid embarrassment, he gave me a lesson in the basement corridors of the SkyDome. My pitch under pressure wasn't mortifying, but neither was it a fine athletic moment.

Much of this activity was fun, but everyone treated me like an A-list celebrity, which sometimes made me feel awk-ward at events I attended with my fellow Olympians. They too were national heroes, but I was always the one whom organizers invited to speak, whom the media wanted to inter-view and around whom people would crowd, asking for auto-graphs. I made a point of acknowledging the rest of the team and their achievements, but the unique pressures on me to meet dignitaries, along with the other hoopla, made me feel separated, not part of the group—a group that included John.

★   ★   ★

I had been named Canadian Female Athlete of the Year in 1991 after winning gold at the World Championships, and now I received that same honour again in 1992. Few athletes have sponsors, so I felt lucky to have had Brooks, Toshiba and Subaru even before Barcelona, and now my higher public profile also allowed me to secure several more sponsorships, including McDonald's, and to upgrade my cute little Subaru Justy to a Subaru Outback. It also meant chances to give key-note speeches, appear on behalf of my sponsors and speak at charity events. I relied heavily on Elliott and his team to manage my schedule, and as a single sculler who likes to be in control, I spent plenty of time with him and the others learning how to move a potential sponsorship along, and how to make my speaking engagements more effective.

I was also given unusual opportunities to do radio and television interviews, to commentate at sports events and to address audiences as varied as high-school students and inter-national entrepreneurs. As comfortable as I am with meet-and-greets, the sheer volume of that first wave of attention was overwhelming. Sharon Podatt from Landmark, who always accompanied me to appearances, became very effective at reading when I'd had enough of a cocktail party or of signing autographs. At one event, where I'd been signing for two hours straight, she noticed I was becoming a little shorter with fans and zoning out, so she cut off the session. After some time alone in my hotel room, then a two-hour workout, I was ready to meet yet another couple of hundred people over dinner.

I'm both an introvert and an extrovert. I love meaningful one-on-one conversations and being in a high-energy crowd. I love hearing people's stories, and I was gratified to discover how much my Olympic victory had meant to them; however, I learned that I do have a limit, which I needed to respect so as not to become grumpy with some well-wisher. It just isn't normal to say hello to two hundred people in an hour. Even while I was becoming more assured in front of the cameras and better able to synthesize ideas, trying to make small talk at receptions continued to exhaust me. Compounding the problem was the trouble I was having hearing in a crowd and against background noise. At an early-morning breakfast for the Special Olympics, I knew I was catching only about every third word, so I just kept nodding and smiling. One woman came up to me later to repeat her question: "I just wanted to know where you bought your beautiful outfit." That jolted me into wondering how many other specific questions had received only a vague nod of my head.

The pace was relentless. As well as doing some international travel, I would fly from Victoria to Toronto once every six days or so, often arriving at 9:30 p.m., then being unable to fall asleep until 2 a.m. because of the time change. At 5 a.m., I'd shiver with fatigue as I showered, then jump around my hotel room to fully wake myself up. Though I was always prepared for each presentation, my schedule infringed on the hours and hours I would have liked to invest in each. After I decided to eliminate the podium and reading from written speeches—so that I instead talked to my audience more casually, using only a few cue cards—I became even more nervous. The first time I tried it, I could hear my voice shaking, but I forced myself to continue, even though I knew my message wouldn't be as polished as I had hoped. Because I still cared then too much about what people thought of me,

I'd beat myself up for my nervousness, for a less-than-stellar performance or for failing to understand my audience, if I felt I'd somehow missed the mark.

I remember one disastrous speech I made at a sports awards banquet in Montreal. I was so dizzy with exhaustion that I was unable to finish it. Afterward, I was holed up in my hotel room when Mark Tewksbury, the amazing Olympian swimmer from Calgary, arrived at my door in his sweatpants. Mark had written to me when I was in the hospital in Germany, creating an instant bond between us even though we hadn't yet met. Later, in Barcelona, where he won Canada's first gold medal of those Games, I had grown very close to him. Mark had wisdom beyond his years, and his delight for life was infectious. We were a lot alike—enthusiastic, playful and a little hyper—so it was great to find this kind of friendship, especially since I was often so lonely.

That evening we lay together across the hotel bed, talking about the problem we shared—the clash between our view of ourselves and how others perceived us. Both of us had been showered with flattering accolades until we began to feel like fakes. People were telling me how courageous I was, how inspiring I was in my ability to face difficulties, how I'd changed their lives, yet here I was, the same imperfect person as before Barcelona.

Many people probably experience that moment when they realize they're not who they thought they were, and nor are they the person others perceive them to be. With Mark and me, this confusion was weirdly exaggerated by our being catapulted into a phenomenal situation in which everyone in the country suddenly seemed to know our names. It was good to talk with another athlete who understood first-hand what a frightening state of flux I was in as I struggled to keep up. Mark and I also shared a passion for the art of motivational speaking, which was how both of us planned to make a living. That night, we talked and talked and talked, quickly getting to the crux of our fears, our insecurities, our ambitions.

The pressure of fame was not something I could easily discuss with John. In that first year after Barcelona, he accompanied me to most of my events, and we both had fun, but he didn't enjoy interacting with the media in the same way I did, nor was he offered the same opportunities. One reason may have been that he had retired from rowing after his gold win at Barcelona, whereas I was just taking time out to heal. On countless occasions, people fussed over me, a bronze medallist, sidelining his gold-medal accomplishment.

The more insane the demands on me, and the more the honours piled up, the more fiercely my inner critic, right on cue, ramped up its judgments, insisting that I didn't have anything worth sharing, and that I was becoming arrogant and aloof.

To some degree, this last bit was true. After about a year of craziness, my personality did start to change. I had built a fence around myself for self-protection, and I didn't always know how to take it down when I was with friends. Sometimes it seemed like I was so tapped out that I had nothing left to give. I'm a very outgoing person, but I recharge by being alone. In order to be public, I needed my home and my neighbourhood to be a place where I felt grounded, but now even this was becoming less so. I'd go to a friend's house and an uncle would be dying to meet me, or a neighbour would drop in, or a niece who had just started rowing would need advice. I'd go to a restaurant and the chef's brother would happen to be a gym teacher who wanted an autograph for his class. I was so grateful for their respect, but I felt like I was always on show—when what I craved was downtime. It was a relief to vacation in the United States and Europe, where I could be anonymous and relax, but on my home turf, my career and charitable causes required me to stay public.

I'm not proud of it, but as the months passed, I became so used to being recognized while travelling in Canada that I expected it, along with the special treatment that came with it. If I didn't get an upgrade on my hotel room or I went unnoticed in a public place, I felt slighted. Friends have told me that I kept my humility, and I believe I did in that I didn't think I was better than anybody else, but I was now living in a world of privilege, a world in which I might be offered the prime minister's suite at the Château Laurier or a free ski weekend at Whistler. That kind of heightened attention changes a person. It made me expect more of myself, but it also made me expect more from others.

One of my biggest challenges after Barcelona was turning down invitations. I received requests for causes so worthwhile, with letters so imploring, that I would inevitably say, "We'll try to fit that in." Meanwhile, my schedule was already stretched so thin that these requests would sit in the "maybe" file or become lost. A fundraising project for cancer survivors in Sudbury, a visit to the Hospital for Sick Children in Toronto, addressing my high school's graduating class, speaking at a rowing club dinner, a request from my first rowing coach—all were engagements I really wanted to accept.

Unfortunately, I was in a double bind. If I said yes too many times, I lost my grounding and was not at my best at any event. If I said no, I felt I was letting people down.

One thing I didn't miss was rowing. I didn't miss the cold, the exhaustion and the reality of always being wet with sweat or waves or rain. It was nice to have a break from the endless routine, and the stress of pushing my body to the extreme.

Despite the many doubts and confusions I experienced, the most lasting feeling I took from Barcelona was one of gratitude. I was so grateful that I was able to pull that race together on that sunny day in Spain. I was so grateful for the people who made my recovery and retraining possible—my wonderful coach, my boyfriend, my doctors, my family and all the friends and teammates who stepped up and took care of me like family. I was equally grateful to the people who gave me shelter, who drove me everywhere, who helped change my bandages, who made me laugh, who lifted my spirit at a time when I was too helpless to look after myself. It's such a comfort to know that those who love you will carry you when you can't walk. Because I was used to relying on my own strength to get through almost anything, that was a huge insight for me—and a blessing during a rocky period of my life.

I also carried with me the conviction that something magical helped me win that bronze medal. I can't rationally explain how I was able to push myself through so many of the physical limitations caused by my massive injury and inadequate conditioning. My belief that I could do it played a huge part in propelling me forward, but I also believe I was aided by something more—a power that revealed itself throughout my recovery and showed up once again in those final metres in

Barcelona. To be physically able to pass Anne Marden so late in the race, when my muscles had long since stopped firing optimally and my lungs were screaming for oxygen, made no rational sense, nor did my feeling that I was lifted over those last metres and carried across the finish line.

I knew my Olympic story would be inspiring, but it took years for me to realize how universal were the lessons I had learned.

In the early days following Barcelona, I often addressed corporate Canada, speaking pragmatically about setting goals, believing in yourself, team building and being accountable. I still use those themes today, but my message has grown more personal and more authentic through a deeper knowledge of myself and of the mysterious powers all around us.

Before my injury, healing had always seemed to be something physical that doctors did for you. During much of my recovery, I thought that I was just going about the business of being an athlete. Athletes visualize. Athletes set goals and push forward regardless of obstacles. It only slowly dawned on me that healing was an attitude, and that it wasn't just about physical recovery or about responding physically to a crisis. The power of the mind and the spiritual forces surrounding us are always there for us to use, day to day, moment to moment, in every situation. If we find ourselves full of self-doubt, or if we want to accomplish something new that frightens us, we can access these powers. Healing is a mindset, not just a physical process.

These kinds of realizations were still in my future, and often discovered through the feedback I received from my audiences, who were eager to share their personal experiences of dealing with loss. Though I didn't always understand what exactly I was doing, I held my bronze medal in my hand as tangible proof that something mysterious had happened in Barcelona, and it gave me the courage to stand up before people to share with them my story.

I had found my new calling.

Part II

MELTDOWN

COUPLING

John and I had our first kiss beside the rabbit cages at the 1988 Summer Olympics in Seoul.

The Seoul compound was an ugly, sterile place constructed of concrete, with nature targeted as the enemy. Twice a day, it was sprayed to eliminate any germs. Instead of cotton sheets, athletes were issued medical ones made of paper. For someone like me, who longs to feel the earth beneath my feet, this environment was very stressful. The rabbit cages seemed to have been installed by the Koreans to cut the odds of our dying of a nature deficit. The two of us gravitated there.

John had captured my attention the night before his last race. At age twenty-four, he was six foot four, with a strong body. His boyish freckles, pale blue eyes and curly brownish-blond hair made him very good-looking in a cute way. A bunch of us were hanging out in the television room, and I asked him how he was feeling about stroking the men's eight the next day. He spoke candidly about his nervousness, then deflected my attention to his teammates, for whom he expressed great admiration. I loved his gentle way of speaking, his lack of bravado and his generosity. Both of us knew we'd made a connection.

Unfortunately, the whole Canadian rowing team bombed that year in Seoul. Not much expertise or money had been invested in our training, and it showed. I was racing doubles with Kay Worthington. Kay's an extremely powerful woman and so am I. Individually we were dynamite. We should have been world-beaters, but as two alpha women, we couldn't find a place where we totally trusted each other. I now realize how arrogant and immature I was in thinking I was better because I had consistently beaten her. Today, I would handle the same situation much differently. So would the coaches, who likely would call in a sport psychologist. I was also in great pain from a back injury that had become chronic, and despite my confident, extroverted facade, I had not yet come to any peaceful sense of who I was.

John's men's eight was the only Canadian entry to make it into the finals, and then they finished last. When the two of us spoke after that, it was over many, many glasses of gin with Gatorade. John saw my massive insecurity about my poor performance with Kay, for which I blamed myself, along with my neediness, and he was not threatened or turned off by it. He gave me constant reinforcement, which must have been exhausting for him. I could see that he was a kind person, well grounded, even-tempered and solid—someone I could rely on, which was very important to me. At twenty-three, I was a lightning bolt with a passion for life that could be contagious, which was probably what John found appealing in me. As well as our mutual love for rowing, we always found other interesting and significant things to talk about.

After only a few conversations, and that kiss by the rabbit cage, we were a couple.

By the end of the Seoul Games, I had begun to believe he was *the* guy. When we were saying our goodbyes, I tried to be casual by telling him, "I hope we see each other again."

After that, I went off for two weeks with five friends on a vacation through South Korea and then Malaysia. Everywhere we went—restaurants, temples—Korean bodyguards followed us. As rowers, we were so bloody tall, like giants, whereas our suit-sporting guards were short, making our group amusingly conspicuous. It was only when we went on a three-hour hike up a mountain that we temporarily lost them. They waited at the bottom, smoking cigarettes.

From Malaysia, I flew to Toronto, arriving at my dad's place in Mississauga at about four in the afternoon. At about 9 p.m. I called John, who was staying with his sister in downtown Toronto. He said, "Why don't we get together now?" Apparently, John had also decided I was *the* girl.

Our relationship moved quickly after that. Like most other athletes jumping from university into the future, neither of us had a place to live or any employment. In the fall of 1988, we rented an apartment together in Toronto's Trinity-Bellwoods area. We used an ironing board as our kitchen table. Both of us were carded, meaning that we each received $650 a month in assistance from Sport Canada as rowers who ranked in Canada's top four. After I'd worked a few months at the Ontario Science Centre, I landed a job with a modest salary as a junior publicist for Penguin Books. John joined McNeil Pharmaceutical, where he earned great money as a sales rep, with the bonus of a company car.

After six months, we moved into an apartment in the High Park neighbourhood, where we settled easily and comfortably into the basics of coupledom. As well as the early romantic *wow!* factor, we were best friends, eager to plan our future. We wanted to excel as Olympians. We wanted to buy a house together. We wanted successful careers after the Olympics.

I adored John's family. His mother, Moira, and his father, Jack, were kind, gracious people who had both been teachers but were now retired. Their door was always open, and whenever we turned up, they would drop everything to prepare a meal to share with us. Jack read incessantly, so he and I usually had lots to discuss. Whereas many of my family members were either estranged from or indifferent to each other, John's uncles and aunts, grandparents and cousins, often met at family get-togethers. Jack and Moira's relationship created a solid, stable family unit, in comparison to my parents' complicated divorce. I immersed myself in John's family, with Moira as my dream mother. We saw the Wallaces most weekends, and they became an important part of my safe place.

One day as I sat looking through old Wallace photo albums, I was surprised to discover a picture of me as a teenager. Apparently, John and I had competed at the same track meets, where his father had officiated. It seemed romantic that we had existed in parallel worlds all those years ago, future partners, circling around the same asphalt without ever meeting. We also had something else in common: my greatest competitor had been Paula Schnurr, who later represented Canada in track at the Olympics. John's guy to beat had been Paula's brother.

* * *

In August 1990, John and I made a huge, life-altering decision. Juggling full-time work with training for the next Olympics had proved to be incredibly challenging. After months of discussion, we quit our jobs. We packed and stacked all our worldly possessions into and on top of our new red Honda Civic, then drove across the country to Victoria. A few days into our trip, the car stank so much we had to stop and unpack everything. We discovered a half-full carton of now sour milk left there by a teammate whom we used to drive to rowing practice, his six-foot-six frame coiled in the back. This was an inauspicious beginning, but we knew exactly what we were doing, where we were headed and why. The lure drawing us west was Mike Spracklen, the newly hired head coach for Canada's men's rowing team.

Before the fall of the Berlin Wall in November 1989, coaches had rarely changed countries. After the fall, all that Eastern-bloc expertise, much of it based on physiology, became available across borders. This was quickly transforming Olympic sport globally, making for a more level playing field. Suddenly, Canada was hiring coaches from Poland and Hungary and East Germany. Though Mike was British, he had worked with the best in the world, including Steven Redgrave, the greatest rower of our time. When John and I heard he was coming to Canada, we could hardly believe our good luck. I instantly decided that he was going to teach me, never mind that he had been hired as the men's coach.

I had a chance to make my case when Mike came to Toronto to meet with the men's eight team and I tagged along with John. Since I had already been training with some of the men in Mississauga, my being at the meeting didn't seem too odd.

At age fifty-two, Mike was a gentle man who looked more like a university professor than a coach. He had a soft voice and spoke carefully, and he had an aura about him that drew people in. You wanted to hear what he had to say, and when he talked about rowing, you had the sense that this man knew what it took to win. I was impressed by the pointed way in which he made the meeting about the athletes, rather than about himself. I had the feeling that following his path might be the most important journey of my life.

When Mike came over to speak with John, he asked me bluntly, "Why are you here?"

I made my pitch using all the logic and passion I could muster, trying to convince Mike to coach me. By then, I'd won bronze in doubles at the 1984 Olympics in Los Angeles. I'd also come fourth in single sculls at the 1985 World Championships in Belgium, before being sidelined with a back injury. Now I pulled out all the stops in my effort to show Mike how much I wanted to win the single, and how much I needed his help.

Mike didn't promise to coach me, but he did invite me to hang out at his BC training camp. That was good enough for me, so John and I headed west. We joined Mike's camp in March 1990, then decided to move out west permanently that August. We rented an apartment in downtown Victoria, supported by the $650 a month each of us was still receiving from Sport Canada. From then until the Barcelona Olympics in 1992, it was practise, practise, practise. Our venue was Elk Lake, connected to Beaver Lake in a provincial park near Victoria and encircled by a splendid ten-kilometre trail that I often hike today.

Mike worked most intensely with the men's eights and sometimes with the men's pairs. I joined them when they were in the smaller singles and pairs boats. Mike would give me a lead on the men off to one side, and I would struggle as valiantly as I could to hold off that inevitable moment when the first boat passed me. Because I was a guest on their playing field, I made an effort to stay out of the guys' way while still taking my place as a teammate. Though Mike was being paid to focus on the men, he often joined me for a few kilometres of my warm-down to instruct me on technique. I was willing to take what I could get, and we quickly made such a strong connection that I never felt like I was being served leftovers. I was hungry to learn and rapt with attention. Mike was endless in his passion for rowing and generous in sharing his knowledge with those who would give themselves to it. He not only could spot talent but also knew who had a tiger's heart, and he nurtured them. Since Mike was focused on athletes who could win, many were not given the gift of his time or talents, but for those of us who were, it was an extraordinary experience.

Mike and I developed such respect for each other that we scarcely needed language to communicate. Perhaps the fact that I had chosen him and working with me was optional made our relationship more special. In those early months, a day never passed in which I failed to learn something profound about the sport I had been training in for six years. Each session was intoxicating in its intensity. No matter how much I absorbed, I knew I was just scraping the surface in discovering what it meant to row. Mike had lived the sport for fifteen years and he was still learning, too.

My favourite time of day that first summer was about 5:30 p.m., when the sun was starting to soften and I would collapse on the dock, along with some of the men. Our bodies heavy with fatigue, we relished the tranquil beauty of the lake, its beauty heightened by the wonderful sense of accomplishment we felt at having survived another day. We knew that what we were doing was insane—six hours a day of training with our heart rates often above 150. Each day we climbed the mountain that was our workout schedule, ending in this peaceful valley, only to climb the mountain again the next day.

Sometimes one of us would start to laugh, a giddy laugh of exhaustion. Others would join in, until we were all laughing. At other times, someone would start talking and the rest of us would add our thoughts before slipping back into silence to stare up at the sky, bonded together in a tender reverie. These were the sweet moments that, however fleeting, kept us going.

On the water, our camaraderie had an entirely different expression. I wanted to come as competitively close to any of the men's boats as I could, and if I could beat one, all the better. It was nothing personal, but if a boat was beside me, I would do everything in my power to stay with it or even pass it. The guys felt the same about each other, but with me they had the added incentive of not wanting to be beaten by a woman. Not that I did that very often. These men were fast, and they significantly outweighed and outpowered me; yet sometimes my experience in the single balanced the differences, so that for a piece, or for twenty strokes, or for a workout, I was able to keep up. Coming close to these powerful men made me feel stronger and built my confidence. In so many ways, this was a perfect situation for me. I could work like a crazy woman to stay beside a men's boat without feeling the pressure to win in order to make the team. Five or six of the men, including John, were unquestionably the best, so for them it was a matter of focusing on the ultimate vision of winning Olympic gold. For the other six or eight male rowers, it was always a dog fight for the last two seats. With so little skill difference between them, there was no room for error.

After about eight months of training, competing and socializing, I was accepted by the other rowers as one of the guys. An encouraging word thrown my way by any one of them would carry me through the day. I came to understand that it was the same for them. I could make a difference not just by how I conducted myself on the water but by what I gave to others in the group. When I arrived early at the boat-house, enthusiastic for the work ahead, a little of that rubbed off on those around me. I tried to compliment them at every opportunity, knowing the burst I got from kind words. On mornings when I was groggy with aching muscles, seeing Andy Crosby antic his way through the boathouse or hearing Rob Marland cheerfully greet everybody made me a little less tired. I loved those guys. I thought they were wonderful. We had lunch together, we had dinner together, we went to the movies together. On Sundays, we hung out at one another's houses together. Rowing and its camaraderie defined my relationship with John, who remained my safe place—someone who would always stand up for me and very patiently listen to me bare all my insecurities.

In two years of intensive coaching, Mike transformed Canada's rowing team from a group of also-rans to world-beaters. After missing the podium in Seoul in 1988, our men's eight would go on to win gold at Barcelona in 1992. After I placed fourth at the World Championships in 1985, then fell to seventh in 1988, Mike took me to silver in 1989 and gold in 1990. After that came all the drama of my bronze in Barcelona in 1992. It was quite a ride, with John and me pacing and supporting each other throughout the journey.

In the four years from Seoul to Barcelona, John and I spent almost every hour of every day together. Our relationship seemed both smooth and solid. Just as we'd planned, we bought a house together in a quiet, old residential area on Cordova Bay—a community I'd really enjoyed a decade before when billeted there while trying out for the National Rowing Team. We adopted a golden retriever named Banner, whom we both adored; together, it felt like the three of us were a little family. And so it wasn't a leap for John and me to talk about marriage. We were already living together, we loved each other, and we saw our future together, so why not?

John formally proposed by taking me out onto Brentwood Bay in a small rented motorboat, where he gave me his grandfather's gold ring. We were married on September 24, 1993. We kept the wedding small, just fifty guests, including our rowing buddies. The ceremony was held outside at Marilyn and Peter Copland's beautiful home, and conducted by my sister's husband, David, a United Church minister. It was a gorgeous day. I wore a cream-coloured, ankle-length silk dress, and John and I passed under an arch of crossed oars as we walked down the aisle together after being married. A four-piece string quartet played, and for the reception everyone strolled along the oceanfront to the Seaview, a tacky but charming little restaurant with vinyl-covered benches. I had been a bit nervous about the politics of the wedding—how our families would get along, who would be invited and who would not—but it proved to be a joyful event.

The wedding took place on a Friday. On Monday, I had to fly to Toronto to deliver a keynote speech. John and I had organized the wedding around my bookings, and while my Toronto keynote assured our honeymoon would be paid for, it made for an abrupt ending to a beautiful weekend. Sadly, my fall schedule became busier and busier, and we never did get to go on our honeymoon.

By now settled in our new home, John and I began to look to the future. Before, we'd kept our finances on separate if parallel paths, but now we talked about "our" money. I was travelling extensively as a public speaker, and John was commuting weekly to Vancouver, where he shared an apartment with his brother, to work in corporate sales for the Unitel phone company. Since his financial rewards were outpaced by the inconvenience, he decided to set up his own business in Victoria renovating houses. When that didn't prove as profitable as he had hoped, he got his real estate licence.

In 1994, I went into training for the 1996 Olympics in Atlanta. In my year off, much had changed. To my delight and dismay, Mike had accepted a position with the American men's rowing team. I was happy for him, but I didn't connect as well with my new coach, Brian Richardson. Brian seemed to have too many athletes for the time available, and following on the heels of my cherished relationship with Mike, I felt uninspired and frustrated. At the World Championship that year in Indianapolis, I won my semifinal and was favoured to win gold—that is, until I double false-started and was eliminated.

The starting procedure had been revised the summer I dropped out, and I hadn't changed with it. I was hard-wired to jump, and when one participant false-started, I reacted. Then I did the same thing a second time. I wasn't the only one—the Championships were marred by sixty flase sarts overall at that regatta. The rules were changed back after one season, but that didn't help me in Indianapolis. I was demoralized. It was such an awful way to end the season. I wasn't feeling well grounded, and I kept beating myself up, telling myself that I'd made this happen because I didn't really want to race.

Luckily for me, Mike was on the dock when I was eliminated, and he knew exactly what to say to comfort me. It must have taken a lot of guts for him to leave the American camp, where he was readying his men's eight, to be the first to meet a sobbing Canadian athlete he hadn't coached in almost two years. This reminded me of how willingly and fearlessly Mike had always stood up for his athletes. That day on the dock, he invited me to train with him in San Diego. He hadn't received permission from USRowing, nor had he thought about how this might inconvenience him. He just saw that I needed his help; he offered it, and I grabbed the lifeline.

Mike's invitation and my acceptance were unpopular on both sides of the border. Mike had to explain to his American bosses why he was coaching a Canadian, while Doug Hamilton, head of Rowing Canada, had to fight for my right to choose my own training program.

Commuting to San Diego made for a frustrating period in my marriage. John was struggling to make a go of his real estate business, and I was missing him terribly after all those years we'd trained together. So we decided that John would set aside his career in order to spend more time with me in San Diego. It was great having him next to me, providing me with emotional support, never mind helping with the daily errands. But I was very consumed and self-centred with my training, and I think John was having difficulty understanding and expressing what he wanted and needed. I could sense something was amiss but couldn't figure out how to help him, or how to be less needy myself. Though he was 100 percent behind me, he seemed a little lost. At the same time, being in San Diego allowed John more time to figure out the bigger questions about what he wanted to do with his life.

Tough and confusing as all this was for me, nothing could compare with the emotional devastation that I experienced in March 1995 at the Pan-American Games in Argentina, indisputably the lowest point of my rowing career.

That trip to South America was supposed to be fun. I had agreed to race in the quads, as well as in single sculls. The Americans would be the only other powerhouse in the competition, and I knew the Canadians would dominate them.

Before leaving for Argentina, I caught a terrible cold. I was coughing so much in our team boathouse that the team doctor suggested I take Benadryl. The over-the-counter antihistamine would help prevent a worsening of my congestion during the flight, he said. Since I'd never before taken a cold medication, I didn't at first follow his advice; however, during our stopover in Toronto for a press conference, I decided to pick some up. When the pharmacist asked what kind of Benadryl I wanted, I told him it was for congestion.

I took one pill on the flight to Argentina, then five days later rowed my single sculls race. I won gold by an obscene margin. As usual, I provided a urine sample to be tested for banned substances. It came back negative. No problem.

My cold continued to bother me, and my coughing was keeping awake the other three competitors with whom I was sharing a room. Then I remembered my medication. Just to be on the safe side, I checked with another of our team doctors to make sure Benadryl was okay.

I had caught him running between patients and hadn't brought the package with me. He said it was fine. Even though the pharmacist had alerted me to the fact that there were different types of Benadryl, I never thought to confirm that mine was the right one.

Feeling secure, I took another Benadryl that night and quickly fell asleep.

In the next day's race, our Canadian quad—Marnie McBean, Diane O'Grady, Wendy Wiebe and me—easily won gold with an eleven-second margin over the Cuban boat. Once again, I routinely provided a urine sample for testing, before flying home to Victoria. I had barely unpacked my bags when I received an agitated phone call from Carol Anne Letheren, CEO of the Canadian Olympic Association. Her words chilled me: "You've tested positive for a banned substance."

I was stunned. My first thought was: *Did someone spike my water bottle?* Then, a few minutes later, as if hit by lightning, I remembered the Benadryl.

John checked the package's label. "I think this might be it," he said.

"How can that be?" I protested. "It was prescribed by one team doctor and confirmed by another!"

I knew that once the media got this story it would be huge,

so I left our house to lie low at the Coplands'. Sure enough, by evening, a helicopter was circling overhead.

My positive test was still just a rumour. Both the Argentina authorities and the Canadian Olympic Association were trying to keep the information under wraps, as there was some question as to whether the substance I had inadvertently taken should actually be on the banned list. It was also clear to the testers that my mistake had been an innocent one— one that perhaps could be dealt with by a quiet warning. I was told not to talk to the media until a decision was made. That's when the worst happened: someone at the Argentina lab leaked the information. Why? I can only speculate. If our team lost gold, Argentina would be bumped up to bronze.

Not speaking to the media during those critical first twenty-four hours once rumours began to circulate was a big mistake. Given my habitual accessibility, saying "No comment" opened the door to every kind of speculation. The story of my "cheating" was front-page news for a week: "Silken: Sneezy or Dopey?" This in turn led to suspicions that my "unbelievable" bronze-medal performance at the 1992 Olympics might have been drug-inspired. I was in shock and in tears all the time, and I couldn't sleep. It was so crushing because I knew I hadn't cheated, and I was still trying to piece together what had happened. I was on the phone to everyone imaginable: the Canadian Olympic Association, Rowing Canada, teammates, coaches, friends. *Would we be stripped of our Pan-American gold medals for the quad? Would I be suspended from competition?* And, of course, the media were constantly calling.

Finally, I did what I should have done in the first place: I held a press conference in which I related exactly what had happened, including that I had checked with team doctors about taking Benadryl in general. Some types of the medication did not contain the banned substance pseudoephedrine, and some did. I had taken Benadryl Allergy Decongestant, the type of Benadryl that did. When a reporter asked if I was angry with the doctors who had approved it without warning me or checking the label, I said that I was. That was another mistake: it was interpreted as a betrayal of them.

If I had it to do again, I would take total and immediate responsibility for the whole fiasco, but at the time I didn't feel responsible because education around drugs in our sport was limited, and I was naive about how someone could cheat without knowing it.

Benadryl contains pseudoephedrine, which is an upper and was banned, as well as diphenhydramine, which is a downer. The diphenhydramine would have cancelled out any charge the pseudoephedrine could have given me. If anything, the Benadryl would have made me drowsy. Shortly after my experience, pseudoephedrine was taken off the banned medication list. Nevertheless, rules were rules, and my quad teammates and I were stripped of our gold medals. I apologized to Wendy and to Diane, and they were very understanding. Wendy even assured me that it could have happened to any one of us, and that she felt sorry about everything I'd had to go through.

I couldn't bring myself to apologize to Marnie McBean. I had enormous professional respect for her, yet our relationship had always been antagonistic, and we had butted heads throughout the regatta. I think Marnie was resentful that I never called her, which was justified, but I was in an emotional crisis and not behaving as my best self or with my highest wisdom. Years later, I did apologize because I realized that I still held anger toward her, and I wanted to put that completely behind me. I told her that I was sorry we had such a negative relationship, and that I wished her only success and happiness. She responded well, and that instantly took the charge out of our relationship.

In the wake of the positive test, I was not suspended from competition, but I was strongly tempted to retire. A reputation is a fragile thing, and after a double false start followed by a doping scandal six months later, I felt like I had three strikes against me. Not wanting to be a quitter, I competed in the 1995 World Championship in Finland, where I won silver, followed by another silver at the 1996 Olympics in Atlanta.

That silver Olympic win, after such a prolonged period of loss and self-doubt, provided a wonderful finale to my rowing career. When journalists suggested that I must be disappointed at never capturing Olympic gold, I could honestly say that I was proud of how I had fought through two major crises of confidence to emerge stronger for the experience. Though I felt some sadness at not hearing "O Canada" played as I stood on the Olympic podium, I can also say that given the chance to race my 1996 final differently, I couldn't imagine a better strategy, or where I could have pushed harder. I knew I had given everything, not only that day in Atlanta but every day leading up to it. My medal was the wrong colour, but I was proud of myself. It was the perfect way to finish my career.

* * *

My transition from the adrenaline rush of Olympic sport to "civilian" life was accomplished with more relief than pain. Unlike so many other athletes, I had no problem finding other goals to be passionate about. For one thing, I had my burgeoning career as an inspirational speaker. For another, I became pregnant.

Right after the Atlanta Olympics, John and I decided to start a family. Since I was thirty-two and wanted more than one child, I knew there was no time to waste. I found out I was pregnant in the second week of October, just nine weeks after the Games, giving me something new on which to focus—though I wasn't always happy about it. I tried to keep up my speaking engagements, but I was very nauseated throughout November and feeling depressed because of that. Some women seem to blossom and glow during pregnancy. I wasn't one of them. I felt fat and out of shape despite continuing to exercise, and I complained a lot. I hated not seeing my hip bones. I hated ballooning so that I couldn't see my feet when I looked down.

On June 20, the day our baby was due, I went to see my doctor. "Well, where is he?"

The doctor sighed. "I knew you'd be like this!"

Every hour I was overdue, I kept thinking, *He's gaining another ounce.* I was already huge, and I suspected that this baby was no lightweight.

I went into labour on June 21. I'd planned to give birth at home with two midwives, but after eighteen hours it became clear the baby would not be coming happily or easily. At the hospital, I was given oxytocin and an epidural to induce contractions, and the baby started to descend, though not into the birth canal. Apparently, this is common enough with highly trained athletes who have an unusual amount of musculature for the baby to push through. Also, he was sunny side up, with his back on my spine, instead of flipped over on his stomach. After five hours of his head emerging and then disappearing again, the obstetrician attempted to pull him by suction. That didn't work, and so my medical team made an emergency forceps delivery on June 23.

When the doctor put my son into my arms—slimy and half blue, with a misshapen head—I thought he was the most beautiful creature I'd ever seen, and John was so excited he started to cry. Without question, the concentration I'd learned as an athlete had helped me to relax into the pain so I didn't become hysterical during the thirty-three hours of labour; it also helped prevent me from collapsing in exhaustion at the finish. This was, however, an entirely different kind of pain from that inflicted by my accident or the overexertion of Olympic training, and when I saw William, I wasn't at all surprised by the difficulty of the delivery. He was shockingly large—an Olympic baby at nine pounds. I didn't understand how he could have fit inside my body.

The moment I took William into my arms, my whole world shifted. I knew from his first breath that he would move me more deeply than any human had done before. I was still too naive to understand that in becoming a parent, I had taken the greatest risk of my life, and that my future happiness would depend on navigating whatever emotional minefield this nine-pound wonder would take me through. Even when he kept me up all night with his crying, or insisted on being nursed every hour, that chunky little boy was utterly perfect in my eyes—except why couldn't he have arrived two pounds lighter?

* * *

As well as having this glorious baby, John and I had purchased a new home on a gorgeous one-and-a-half-acre property on Cordova Bay. The1938 farmhouse had an upstairs that lacked full ceiling height and additions that had been tacked on in an ad hoc way. Working alongside a contractor, John stripped the old farmhouse down to its bones and began the renovation. The weekend before William was born, I lugged a heavy, borrowed handmade wooden cradle upstairs into the bedroom, where John and I slept on a mattress on a metal frame. But we were ready for the baby!

Within three months I had exercised myself back to my normal 165-pound weight. William was a good baby, though he continued to be hungry all the time. Since John and I were both working, we respected that each of us needed our rest. John was a great partner with cooking and cleaning, and a very hands-on father when it came to changing diapers and getting up at night and in the early hours of the morning when I couldn't handle William's demands. We also had a series of nannies; they sometimes travelled with me when I took William along. Even Banner, our golden retriever, loved the baby.

I was pondering whether I would return to rowing for the Sydney Games in 2000 when I became pregnant again. I think I allowed that to happen because I'd already decided to retire, but this "surprise" was how the situation formally worked itself out.

Kate was born on November 4, 1999, some two years and four months after William. She arrived on time; she was eight pounds, with a tiny head, and it all happened within eight or nine hours. This time I was more prepared for how a new baby would rock my world. To begin with, it upped the ante in terms of running our household. I had already hired Pinky Condor, a nanny from the Philippines who would also help with the housework. She arrived a day early—so that I came home from the hospital to a freshly cleaned home and folded socks—and instantly became a crucial part of our family.

When I first held Kate, a part of me wondered how my emotional vulnerability could become any more intense. She was just as needy as William, but in a completely different way. Whereas he was always hungry, Kate exhibited a constant desire to move. She came out with one arm waving to the world and was so active that, after a year, she had only doubled her birth weight. She was the baby I couldn't breast-feed while having a conversation because she would whip her head off the nipple to try to join in. She controlled the household from the first moment she let out her ear-piercing scream, causing William to whimper, "Please, Mommy, make her stop." As if I could. I had no more control over her screaming than anything else she wanted to do. She was, and is, a force of nature, and I loved every smart, driven, hyper ounce of her, even when John and I, out for dinner with friends in Montreal, received a call from our babysitter begging us to return to our hotel.

Kate walked at eight months, talked at fourteen months and has kept talking in full, animated sentences ever since. What I had no way of knowing was how completely Kate and

William would redefine the way I saw myself and the world—though I was beginning to receive a few clues. When I looked in the mirror at Silken Laumann, I saw a woman in her thirties, living in a lovely home in a leafy Victoria neighbourhood, with a loving mate of fourteen years, two wonderfully healthy children and a happy dog. John and I were doing quite well financially, and my career as a public speaker was challenging in all the right ways. What could possibly go wrong?

UNCOUPLING

O n Sunday, March 28, 2002, John and I were lying side by side in bed when he suddenly sat up and told me, "I don't think I want to be married anymore."

My shock was total. I asked him to repeat what he had said—it was almost as if my ears were ringing and I couldn't hear him properly.

"I don't think I want to be married anymore." He started to cry.

I was stunned, but my first thought was of William and Kate. Shaking and shivering with emotion, I begged him, "Don't take my kids away."

John left, and we never spent another night together. My world was turned upside down. Everything I'd envisioned for the future was challenged.

Why did John and I separate and divorce after fourteen years of a close friendship, Olympic triumph and the birth of two beloved children? The answer is as complex as the two people in the marriage.

Until the night John left, I had thought our marriage was

a happy one. Though I'd felt John pulling away, I refused to believe we had a serious problem. Maybe I was in denial because I didn't possess the psychological tools that might have enabled me to face—and possibly fix—John's unhappiness and our growing dysfunction. Either way, I felt blindsided.

Two years earlier, when I was pregnant with Kate, John hadn't seemed as engaged as he had been with William's birth, and I'd ceased to know where he was mentally much of the time. He wasn't doing any workouts, he spent many hours at a time on his computer and he always seemed distracted. I also knew he was feeling restless with his career as director of a foundation that created rowing and paddling opportunities for kids, another new venture for him. Instead, he wanted to carve his own future by owning a business.

Before our marriage, John had wondered out loud about whether the greatest moment of his life—his Olympic gold medal—was behind him. We tried to look forward to other incredible moments ahead, but I could understand how any ordinary career—no matter how brilliant—could pale in comparison to the passion and commitment that gets you to the top of the podium. I'd been lucky to have discovered a passion for public speaking, which had filled that void for me, but John hadn't connected with a new passion yet. He had often seemed unhappy, and when I tried to get him to talk about his feelings, he shrugged me off.

The night John moved out, we agreed that we would wait to speak to the children together. The next morning, I simply told William, age five, and Kate, age two, "Dad's gone away to Calgary to visit a friend."

That was no big deal. They were used to both of us travelling. Ten days later, when John returned, we sat down with William and Kate and told them we wouldn't be living together as a family anymore.

It was the hardest speech I've ever had to make. I knew that the feelings John and I shared with William and Kate that day would change their lives forever. From then on, they would have a split family, and there could be no going back to the life we'd known.

Overcome with grief and fear, I called a friend who was a family counsellor. She told me, "Silken, you can't protect your kids from life's pain, but you can equip them to cope."

John rented an apartment downtown while the kids and I stayed in the family home. He could see them there on a regular basis and take them on excursions, but he could not have them for sleepovers because I didn't want them experiencing the upheaval of going from one place to the other. The way I saw it, since he was the one who had quit the marriage, he could be the one inconvenienced.

Initially, John was to put the kids to bed on Tuesdays and Thursdays, while I visited a friend. Because the children had a nanny, our schedules needn't overlap. My Mama Bear instincts were in full arousal, and it seemed crystal clear that this was best for the kids—Kate was still a baby.

John reluctantly agreed.

As soon as William discovered the reality of what our separation meant for him, he became angry with me: "Why isn't Daddy living with us?" "I miss Daddy!" "I don't like you!"

Under the circumstances, these outbursts hurt, but I tried to put them aside. William needed a "safe place," so I allowed him to vent.

About two weeks into our separation, John and I went to see a counsellor. She was someone we'd visited once a few years before to try to help us improve our communication. Then, we'd talked generally about what makes a good marriage, and that had seemed enough. Now, I was hopeful she could help us put our marriage back together again.

But the reality seemed just the opposite: it felt to me like our session was actually designed to help John tell me that his decision to end our marriage was final. I was devastated, and that devastation was compounded by my growing suspicion that John was having an affair.

When John had first told me he was leaving, I had asked if he was involved with someone else, even though a big part of me couldn't believe he would cheat on me. He adamantly denied it, but I could feel he wasn't being truthful with me. We had been through so much together, and still shared so much, including our amazing kids. In the end I had to piece together the narrative from others, who'd seen him at restaurants with a woman who worked with him. When I confronted him, he insisted that he and Jessica were just friends. Later, he admitted they were together *now* but hadn't been while we were married. I was skeptical, but it almost didn't matter, since what was done was done.

Many of our friends had trouble coming to terms with our separation. One exclaimed, "But you had the best marriage of any of us!" Their shock underlined my own. What had gone wrong? Nothing much, as far as I could see. My husband had simply stopped loving me. I wanted this to be somebody's fault, but certainly not mine.

Many friends offered advice. One rowing buddy tried to

explain how my fame and personality had affected John. "It's hard for him to live in your shadow. Couldn't you just tone yourself down—be less 'big'?"

I protested, "It's important for me to have dreams and to always be improving both my outer and my inner lives. Following your advice would be like saying no to who I am, and killing myself one day at a time. I want to become *more* me, more authentic, more courageous, more of a risk-taker. *Less* is denying myself the right to be me."

"See? That's exactly what I mean," he replied. "Everything you say is so motivational."

Though my friend was well-intentioned, my gut told me his advice was not right for me. Many women reduce themselves so as not to threaten a partner, but becoming all we can be is everyone's human journey. If this bumps up against perceptions of who we should be, we need to have the courage to challenge those perceptions.

My friend André Spencer offered to lead John and me in a healing circle with two other counsellors. I had little knowledge of Native teachings, but I had a deep respect for André's life experience. He had been through the hell of being raised in a residential school, and had lived on the streets coping with drug addiction. But he had found the courage to heal his life and was working as a counsellor when I met him. A healing circle was outside anything John and I knew—and I worried John would scoff at passing a feather around a sacred circle and burning sweetgrass; however, I trusted André and so I found the argument that persuaded John: "I think it would help us move forward."

We spent five hours in a little cabin, allowing each person

who held the feather to speak without interruption. André sat between John and me, giving us both time to digest each other's words before responding. I yearned to ask John why he couldn't love me and to specify the exact moment when he had stopped loving me. Instead, I shared my pain, expressed my anger and did a lot of listening. I listened to John's guilt. I listened to a man with no answers. He really didn't seem to know what had gone wrong, which led me to ask myself, *What answer would make it all right for our marriage to be over?*

In the end, we hugged each other and cried.

Even with that resolution, I was left with a hangover of anger. John and I were in a circle of healing and forgiveness, the safest circumstances for telling the truth, yet he had still denied he was seeing someone.

The first six months of our separation were especially rough. Every day I grappled with a crushing sense of failure. Uncoupling was the end of the dream in which both of us had believed when we exchanged our wedding vows. John and I were not going to walk hand in hand into the sunset together. We were not going to weep through our children's university graduations and weddings together. We were not going to buy a winter home in Arizona. We were not going to play with our grandchildren together. We were not going to share memories in our side-by-side rocking chairs in an old age home.

The end of a marriage is a staggering loss, not just of a life partner but of one of the biggest dreams we in this society have. How could I have missed the telltale signs? I remembered wondering that about others who seemed so shocked when their partners left, and I'm ashamed to say I hadn't had much sympathy, thinking, *How could anyone be so deluded, so absorbed in daily trivialities?* Now I was the one with so much sadness, so much anger, so much hurt, so much confusion, trying to say goodbye to John my lover, my friend, my confidant. John my protector, my sweetheart.

At the same time, I was dealing with the practical stress caused by that loss—learning to juggle a daily routine without John there, helping the kids handle the transition, working out the terms of our separation and trying to run my business, which now felt even more necessary for our support. *What if I'm unable to carry the load?*

It was in the evenings, when I was restlessly tossing in our big empty bed, the kids sleeping next door, that I felt unbearably vulnerable. I would check them incessantly, unnerved to have their safety completely in my hands—what if I didn't hear their coughing or choking, or the footsteps of a predator in the house? That's when the love of my closest friends sustained me. Instinctively, they knew that nighttime alone in our big old house would usher in my darkest hours, and they took turns calling to "tuck me in." My friends proved to be pillars of support. We took long walks together; they took me shopping and planned nights away. They took my kids on nights when I was too tired to parent well, and were always present for me with a hug and a cup of tea or a home-cooked meal.

After about six months, John's visiting the children in what was now supposed to be my house no longer worked. When he was present, it seemed like he was back—not just visiting—giving me the awful feeling that I was stuck somewhere between where I had been and where I now was. John began taking the kids for Saturday overnights, and later he would have them every second weekend. When Kate and William left for their first weekend with their dad, my girlfriend Brenda had only to hear my voice on the phone to know that I needed her. She came right over, then embraced me as I cried. Day after day, setback after setback, my friends were there for me.

I took some comfort from the fact that others had confidence in my strength, though unexpected glitches could often derail me without warning. One winter's day, I determinedly packed up wind pants, skis and water bottles for my first cross-country ski trip as the only parent in charge. After driving three hours from Victoria to Mount Washington, I unloaded the kids, helped them with their equipment, then rushed them to their ski group at our designated time.

A ski patroller asked me for their passes.

Where were they? With horror, I realized they were still in the car.

When he insisted on seeing them, I burst into tears, worn out by the effort of organizing these two little people all by myself. Embarrassed and emotionally drained, I took the kids—now insisting they didn't want to ski—back to the car. I packed everything up again and drove us home to Victoria.

Even when our lives were running more smoothly, William was often still angry. He was very young—just six years old—and didn't know how to express his frustration at having two homes, not one. When he came home from seeing John he would be furious with me or sometimes in tears, which I found very hard. I hadn't chosen this for us either, but I found myself coping with this inconsolable little boy. One day he shouted, "I hate you!" before stomping off to his room. My shock was closely followed by a flash of anger: *How dare you talk to me that way?* When I strode after William, he threw a book at me. Since I was holding a plate, I flung it at the wall. After that, we both burst into tears.

I realized then that I was trying so hard not to be angry with John that I was misplacing my rage, directing it at my kids. In fact, I was always so calm and reasonable with John that I no longer knew how I was feeling until my anger seeped out in unexpected and inappropriate ways. After that insight, I usually was able to make the necessary distinctions so that when William came home crying, I could be empathetic in a useful way. Though I couldn't make William's hurt disappear, I could give his emotions space by acknowledging and accepting them by saying things like, "You seem really angry." He would still yell back and occasionally slam doors, but when he was given permission to vent, the time he spent being overwhelmed shrank from a day to hours to less.

Even after turning the corner in my uncoupling, I could still find myself caught off guard by inconsequential things, like the first time I found my bread covered with mould. Before John had left, the two of us would finish a loaf in a week—no mould. Now, each time I trashed another decaying loaf I thought of him.

My brother-in-law, David, the minister who had married us, and one of the wisest, kindest men I know, assured me, "Silken, this too shall pass." Those biblical words gave me the same comfort they've given others for hundreds of years. *This too shall pass.* Some days they served as a mantra, helping me to put one foot in front of the other.

Amidst the pain and confusion, I started to feel an odd sense of possibility. Now that the traditional life of two kids and a husband had vanished, I realized that I could put anything I wanted in its place. New hopes and new dreams were beginning to stir and burgeon inside me. I began to feel lighter. Without realizing it, I had slowly let go of parts of myself that were profoundly important to me through the years I was married. This included both the writer in me and the artist in me. It also meant not allowing myself the solitude that connected me to my inner knowing and to the universal energy that joins each of us to the power that is the Source. I was baffled by how I could have let this happen, though I knew that it happened not all at once but day by day. Now I began to ponder what new things I wanted to include in my life. I wanted to write a book. I wanted a closer relationship with women. I wanted to spend more time with people who were a wee bit eccentric, in the way I used to be. And I wanted to change my physical space to be more reflective of who I was—art on the walls, books on the shelves—while I decided what I would do in this next chapter of my life.

The healing circle with André had been my first attempt to reach out to new disciplines in order to reach down deeper inside myself. I also turned to yoga, which at first I hated. Whereas rowing is about power, strength, aggression and effort, yoga is in many ways about slowing down and softening the body to connect with the spiritual self. After each yoga session, I would cry, even though there was no emotion or event associated with my tears. It was pure physical release. Since I found that intriguing, I kept on attending classes, until I became comfortable using my body as a spiritual channel.

I also started to keep a journal. As a confused teenager, I had used a secret diary to help me sort my heart from my head. Now I gave myself permission to go there again.

★ ★ ★

When it came to formally and legally uncoupling, John believed we didn't need lawyers, and I decided he was right. We were both fair and decent people, weren't we? I didn't want to taste bitterness every time I heard John's name. I didn't want our children to experience anything but caring and respect between their two parents. I hoped we could unhitch our lives like boxcars from a train, then move off in new directions, but I had no idea how to make this happen. I needed wisdom and role models.

The bookstore's self-help section offered a paltry selection of titles whose language reinforced the toxic energy that surrounds divorce in our culture: "wronged party," "alimony," "custody," "divided assets." We heard a lot more of this language of hostility and battle when, at my suggestion, we attended a collaborative law session advertised as the path of least conflict in a divorce. As I sat across from the man I had loved most of my adult life, listening to lawyers tell us how we should sort out our future, I began to shake with rage. Afterward, I raced to my car, John in close pursuit wanting to know if I was all right. The wheels of the car as I pulled away shrieked my response. Assaulted by the images that had been put into my mind of vengeful couples fighting over the kids and stealing money from joint bank accounts, I wanted to scream in confusion and fury. Surely, what I was hearing was irrational. Despite the breakdown of our marriage, I still believed my husband was a kind and loving man. Even so, the apparent reality of those stereotypical blind-with-rage divorcing couples now tainted my thoughts.

With the assistance of our accountant and a few friends, John and I had a legal separation within a year and a divorce two years later, both initiated by me. I was relieved that we were able to uncouple our lives without a legal team, which had taken discipline and control on both our parts. I was also proud that I didn't seem to possess any rancour toward John, and that I consistently did things to make him feel better, like having a quiet fortieth birthday dinner for him and the kids. It was only later that I realized I had buried many of my unsafe feelings to protect John, at a cost to myself and sometimes even to our children.

In truth, I felt a huge amount of pressure. I worried incessantly—not just about working hard to keep our family as normal as possible, but also about working overtime with my speaking commitments so that no matter what happened, I could go to bed at night knowing William, Kate and I were financially secure in our home.

Even when we were both trying so hard to be fair, we did have sticking points. When John asked to be compensated for the family furniture, he hit a raw nerve. I was not going to buy him out of the crystal candlesticks, the broken-spring sofa our children had ruined through jumping or the bed imprinted with his body. I snapped, "Just take whatever you want." I wasn't perfect either: I refused to even consider letting John have our joint share of a recreational property we'd invested in, which John also wanted.

Many times I struggled to pull back from the brink of conflict by reminding myself of my new vision for our family. Maybe it was the yoga and meditation that sustained me. Maybe it was because I collapsed each night into that body-imprinted bed and prayed—for the compassion to continue to love and respect my husband, for the strength to keep my wounded pride from poisoning our separation.

What I most needed was a shared faith that we could still do an outstanding job of parenting our children together while living in separate houses. On William's fifth birthday, when I couldn't assemble the Lego set he'd received as a gift, he became so hysterical that I called John, who arrived within minutes to help. Watching our child struggle with the pieces, hiccuping with tears, screaming with rage, I would have done anything to take away his pain if I could have.

Redefining our family was challenging in unexpected ways. Whereas many separated couples must strive for civility, John and I initially struggled to create healthy boundaries. Sometimes I would stop myself just in time from sharing with him my misgivings about a speech I was writing, remembering that this level of intimacy was no longer safe for me. On those occasions, I learned to consult a colleague instead, or a friend. Not John.

The two of us were not the only ones wrestling with redefinition. At age six, William asked, "Mommy, are you still a wife?" When I replied no, he asked, "Is Daddy still a husband?" Again I said no. After a long pause, he asked, "Are we still a family?"

Remembering the day John came over to help us with the Lego set, I felt comfortable reassuring him, "We will always be a family."

THE BOTTOM

n February 2006, I reached one of the most desperate points in my life: I locked my children in a hotel room to prevent myself from screaming abuse at them or, worse, hitting them.

I had taken them to Phoenix, a holiday for them and a keynote speech for me. William had been whining non-stop for at least a couple of hours about wanting to play on the bigger water slides, even after I'd told him no, and about being hungry. Kate was growing hysterical because she was hungry, too, and because a tag on her bathing suit was chafing her skin. I was feeling tense over not yet having finished the final draft of the next day's speech, and my patience was wearing thinner and thinner. Finally, I snapped. All I could hear was a furious voice in my head demanding that I smack the spoiled brats just to silence their ungrateful voices. *Don't they know how difficult my life as a single mother has become? Don't they know the pressure on me to deliver a stellar speech tomorrow?*

I shrieked "Stop it!" then ran out of the room, horrified that I felt so out of control that I might endanger them. Adrenaline surged through my body. I couldn't stop shaking. I banged my head repeatedly against the hallway wall, hoping to make my terrible rage go away, and hating myself with a new level of ferocity. Who was this monster who couldn't take the ordinary stresses of motherhood? I wanted to ram my entire body into that concrete wall with the force of a Mack truck.

My life was unendurable.

This was not the first time something minor had set me off, filling me with a scary fury that seemed to have no source, and always followed by self-recrimination, self-loathing and depression. I'm the sort of person who finds it hard to ask for help, but that day in Phoenix, I knew I'd hit bottom.

I phoned my friend Kim.

For months, she had been encouraging me to see the counsellor who had guided her through her own battles with anxiety and depression. As she'd watched each day become harder for me, she had anticipated my meltdown. Now she wasn't afraid to tell me the truth, even if I lashed out at her in denial, perhaps ending our friendship.

I made the call to Neil Tubb as Kim so strongly urged— right there, outside my hotel room, on my cellphone, before I lost the courage. I made that call despite feeling embarrassed and ashamed that someone as blessed with good fortune as me needed help. I knew I was generally a good parent, but having to lock the kids in the hotel room clearly demonstrated I was in over my head. I'd been pushing myself to exhaustion, functioning as an overcompensating supermom to protect them from the repercussions of John's and my split, walking them to school each morning, even volunteering for extracurricular school duties. Then I would stay up late, preparing speeches or writing my first book, which was to be published in the spring.

Compounding everything was my years-long struggle with insomnia. Each morning, I would awaken at 2:50, lie wide-eyed until dawn, then perhaps doze for an hour before Kate or William crawled into my bed. I was so tired during the day that I'd fall asleep the moment I sat down anywhere. I lived in terror of conking out while driving.

When John took the kids, I'd be torn between sleeping and enjoying my freedom by celebrating with friends, pumped on adrenaline. Over the years, I'd become more conservative in both my behaviour and dress. Now, with only myself to please, I went dancing with friends and attended amazing parties—I started to feel excited by life and its possibilities.

About five months after my separation, I slept with someone for the first time. It felt amazing to be desired again. After a fourteen-year exclusive relationship, I was rediscovering a hidden part of myself. I felt feminine and sexy, and awake to the reality that I really was single and that I could enjoy sex outside of emotional attachment. These relationships were fun and worked perfectly for me at a time when I was too emotionally spent to want commitment. Most importantly, I didn't want my home to have a revolving door for boyfriends, whose presence might confuse the kids.

And then, I met someone I really cared about.

At first, it was wonderful. He was loving, attentive and kind, and great with my kids, both thoughtful and fun. He was also a very controlling person who saw everything in black and white. I wanted to love him because he was a decent man and he was crazy about me. I also believed he might be my only chance to find another partner. As I told myself, *You have a difficult and complex personality. Shouldn't you feel lucky just to have someone who loves you?*

I spent months trying to convince myself that he was the right guy. When I went away for a few days to think through our relationship, he followed me, arriving at the door with a bouquet of flowers. We decided to try again, but that attempt was a failure. I was too independent for him, and I wasn't willing to give up one inch of my freedom. A part of me wanted to keep believing that I could have it all. "All" meant finding someone with a huge world vision, a big personality and big dreams—a person who was willing to live large, take risks and keep growing. It was a tall order, but finally I realized in my heart of hearts that I couldn't settle for anyone who wasn't the right fit.

It was my tumultuous relationship with this man, as well as the incident with my kids in Phoenix, that made Kim so emphatic about my seeing her counsellor, Neil Tubb. By my first appointment, I'd convinced myself that all I needed was a bit of tweaking—a chance to get a few things off my chest and maybe acquire new coping mechanisms. When Neil asked why I'd called him, I replied casually that a relationship had recently come to a sad but predictable end, and that I was experiencing bursts of rage that scared me. While I blathered on about how good my life was apart from a few stresses, and about how self-aware I had become from reading lots of books, I'm sure Neil must have seen that I was nursing deep issues in desperate need of resolution. After an hour, I made another appointment for two weeks later, still feeling self-conscious, and completely unaware that I'd just initiated a difficult six-year journey into the deepest recesses of my psyche.

During the next couple of sessions, Neil and I addressed my hangover of confusion and regret from my most recent relationship. I also began to realize how screwed up I'd been to keep travelling down the path of intimacy with someone I knew was absolutely wrong for me. Many of my friends had tried to warn me that we weren't suited for each other. My sister had been most emphatic: "Silken, you're kidding yourself. He's *not* the one!" Even while the relationship was at full throttle, I sometimes had the awful out-of-body experience of watching myself almost self-destruct, while asking, *What the hell are you doing!*

Neil helped me to realize that this relationship was simply one that I thought I needed to get me through the fallout from my divorce. Experiencing unqualified love was intoxicating after being abandoned. All the drama of our relationship had also served to stave off my entrenched childhood feelings of not being good enough.

Neil also helped me to better understand my relationship with John. When he and I were rowing together, we appeared to be a lot alike, when in fact we were profoundly different people.

John's kindness and support had been genuine, but by unintentionally enabling my insecurities, he may also have remained detached from his own feelings. My neediness gave him a really big job to do! As I grew more confident with success, I started to feel it was my job to make John happy and secure—to "caretake" him as he had me. Neil taught me that trying to solve another person's problems was disrespectful as well as ineffectual. During our marriage, this self-assigned role also made me guarded about sharing the news of yet another sponsorship or some honour I was to receive. While living with John, I had done a great deal of apologizing for who I was. If John and I were to meet now for the first time, we would never marry because we would know instinctively that we could not give each other what each of us needed. Perhaps it was inevitable that our marriage would end, and John had simply been the one to recognize that first.

Despite these insights, counselling continued to be a difficult concept for me to understand. I'd talk about all this stuff that made me self-conscious—moments in my marriage, moments in my parenting, lies or actions that made me sad or mad or ashamed or even afraid. Often I would think, *Why am I here? Why do I feel so messed up? I've achieved so much— I've created a successful business, I have friends who love me. Am I really enough of a head case to be here? Do I want to go through this process if it's going to hurt this badly? Can I just walk away and be okay?*

Even as I asked myself these questions, the truth was whispering to me out of a deep and enduring sadness as it struggled to find its voice. Beneath that sadness was rage, and beneath that rage was sadness and then another layer of rage. Under all these layers I quivered, quivered with the feeling that underlay all the others: *I may not be worth this effort.*

In about our fourth session, Neil asked me about my childhood. I found his questions upsetting, and I challenged him: "Why do we have to go there? It's such a long time ago."

Neil was firm but gentle. "You have to unravel the past in order to live fully in the present."

Though I resisted this concept intellectually, my heart already knew where I had to go. I tried to get off the topic quickly, or at least to explain my childhood using a framework I'd created a long time ago. "My parents were German immigrants who came here after World War II. They had a lot of really tough problems to deal with, both before and after they emigrated." My dad's voice was strong in my ear as I asserted, "Sure, we had some difficult times in our family, especially around my mom, but my siblings and I always had nice clothes. We lived a normal, middle-class suburban life."

Neil would have none of it. He asked more and more questions, then responded to my offhand descriptions of pivotal childhood events in sympathetic ways that threw me off guard. I would reply, "Yes, but . . ." and then add all sorts of qualifications to make it clear that everything that went wrong between my parents and me was actually my fault.

In the end, it was my little daughter who revealed to me the truth of my childhood and showed me what it means to love myself—Kate, beautiful Kate, with her white-blonde hair, her electric energy and her irrepressible passion. Time after time, I would dismiss little Silken's emotions as inappropriate or irrelevant, until Neil confronted me with this question: "How would you feel if these incidents that happened to little Silken had happened to Kate?"

Kate, my beloved little Kate? Are you crazy? I would protect her with every fibre of my being.

But I had had no compassion for little Silken, only the conviction that if something was wrong with her life, then she must have done something bad. Either that, or she should have figured out what others were doing that made things so scary and awful and senseless, and changed it. Now, when I saw that little Silken at six was just like my little Kate, intelligent and fragile and completely innocent, I crumbled. *How could I condemn with loathing somebody so shy and absolutely vulnerable? Why had little Silken too rarely been allowed to experience the unconditional mother's love I feel for my children? Oh my God, please, Mom, don't hit her. Please don't let her feel everything is her fault! Please don't shut her down or allow her to feel unworthy.*

Before therapy, I was unaware of how profoundly the troubles in my childhood had affected who I was. Or maybe I was simply afraid of opening Pandora's box in case I couldn't close it again or, worse, became trapped inside. I didn't have words to name what had happened to me, because I'd never had cuts or bruises to offer up as proof to the world and to myself. Now, I was beginning to understand that if I couldn't find the courage to name it, the truth was going to kill me. I decided that I really did need help, and that this help would indeed come from this man who asked so many difficult questions, this bearded cherub with a heart as big as an ocean and an edge that comes from having experienced some hard living himself.

I was about to begin my most incredible journey ever— the journey that would teach me to love myself just for being Silken.

PART III

UNRAVELLING THE PAST

MY MOM

One scene from my childhood remains indelibly etched in my mind. I am standing, age six, at the top of the stairs in our house on Narva Court in Mississauga, carrying a beautiful pale blue dress with a navy sash that cascades to the floor. My dad gave the dress to me for my uncle Rolf's wedding, and I utterly love it.

My mom looks angry. I feel confused. I'm so excited about this fairy-tale dress, but my mom's face frightens me. Later, when we're alone, she slaps me. "You're always trying to get your dad to spoil you," she scolds.

I'm ashamed. I know I must have done something wrong, but I don't know what. I want Mom to know what she's saying isn't true, but now doubt has crept in. *Maybe I am bad. Maybe I am trying to steal Dad's attention, like she always says.*

I remember another scene, this time on the day of Uncle Rolf's wedding. My mom poses with one hand on a birdbath and the other on her hip. She is wearing a lovely white, flower-embossed gown with a long light blue train draped around her. On her blonde head she wears a sheer blue veil.

Today, not even Uncle Rolf's bride can escape my mom's need to be in the spotlight.

* * *

My mom, Seigrid Seideman Laumann, was born in Leipzig, Germany, in 1938. When she was a young girl, her father left to serve in the German army. He never returned. The family never received a death notice. He just disappeared. Seigrid had been "Daddy's little girl," whereas her younger sister, Helga, was closer to their mother. Seigrid and her father had shared a talent for the arts. He was her hero. She always hoped the door would open someday and he'd come walking through it.

My parents met in East Berlin in 1959; my dad was twenty-three and my mom was twenty-one. Hans had immigrated to Canada three years earlier, but he had returned to Germany for a visit that stretched into eighteen months. Both he and Seigrid were selling magazines for the same company. With Seigrid's long blonde hair, high cheekbones and classic features, her dynamite figure and slender legs, she was a sexy knockout. Hans was tall, handsome and muscular, with thick brown-blond hair. Both were remarkably passionate young people who had similar backgrounds and were primed for adventure. I have no trouble understanding the magnitude of their attraction to each other.

Since construction of the wall separating East and West Berlin did not begin until 1961, it was still possible for citizens to leave Soviet-controlled East Germany, though illegal to do so. A train connected East and West Berlin, and was patrolled by Soviet police who checked identification papers, but if you were willing to take a risk, it was possible to slip into West Berlin by simply sneaking off at the "wrong" stop and hoping you wouldn't be asked for your papers again. Seigrid left her bags in one of the train cars that opened to a platform in West Berlin. Seconds before the doors opened, she rushed to that end of the train to collect them, then stepped onto the platform, where Hans was waiting for her. They married in a simple civic ceremony, then travelled to Canada.

I can imagine how my mom must have felt arriving in Toronto without knowing anyone or any English. Many Canadians still carried resentment, even hatred, toward Germans for the Nazi war atrocities, and both my parents had thick accents. She must have been terribly isolated and alone.

My dad earned money any way he could, including carpentering and selling Fuller brushes and encyclopedias. Since he could see that self-employment was the best way to secure his family's future, he bought some basic window-cleaning equipment and hired himself out. After months of hard work, he'd earned enough to buy more equipment and to hire another man to work for him. That was the start of Sparkle Window Cleaning, and the beginning of real financial stability for my parents. Soon he and my mom could afford to rent a spacious three-bedroom apartment on Lawrence Avenue in Toronto.

My sister, Daniele, was born in 1961, and I followed on November 14, 1964. Three years later, my parents purchased their first house, a white bungalow on Indian Road in Mississauga, where my brother, Joerg, was born in 1968. It was the smallest house in the nicest of neighbourhoods but still a concrete sign that my parents' dream of making a comfortable life for themselves in Canada was coming true.

Our family moved seven times after that, usually within an eight-kilometre radius—close enough that my Maltese terrier, Bimbo, could chase after the moving van, ears flying. We kept changing houses because my mom always believed the neighbours were spying on us. No matter how pleasant someone might be, in a few months Mom would convince herself that "the British lady" down the street hated Germans and was recording our family's activities. The police came at least once about my mother's interactions with the neighbours, and though I was ushered out of the room while they spoke to my mom, I remember my dad telling her after they left that she couldn't harass the neighbours anymore. It was scary having them come to our door to warn my mom.

The houses my parents chose were often unique in some nifty way—one had an amazing backyard playhouse; another was inspired by Frank Lloyd Wright, its floor-to-ceiling windows overlooking a ravine; yet another was on a private lane with no traffic. However, changing our residence so often further isolated us as a family. I now understand that my mom's behaviour was rooted in her experiences in postwar East Germany, but when I was a kid, all that moving simply frustrated and dislocated me.

In my childhood memories, Seigrid—or Sigitta, as she liked to call herself—was a vibrant, intelligent and beautiful woman who wore elegant clothes and had a penchant for drama. She also possessed a melodic voice with which she could sing, hum or even whistle hundreds of choruses. I remember Daniele and I paddling her across Stoney Lake, where our family sometimes rented a cottage, while she played her guitar and sang. It was easy to see why my dad had married her.

My happiest memories highlight her childlike joy—laughing at the smallest of pleasures, savouring her cup of coffee, bouncing around the living room dancing and singing; her delight at the seafood brunch at the Valhalla Inn; her pleasure at presenting me with some special item of clothing she knew I would like. When I was in grade eight, I desperately wanted a pair of black "China slippers," which were all the rage. After searching every store in Toronto's Chinatown, she found me a pair in size nine.

My mom filled our various houses with the products of her creativity: paintings, wall hangings and sculptures. She studied fine arts at Humber College, and wherever we were living, she would take over the garage or a room as her studio. She also filled our home with books on art and philosophy. This was the 1960s, when the average middle-class, suburban housewife still had a fairly oppressive existence, so it was inspiring for me to have a mother who was passionate about creating something of her own. When we arrived home from school for lunch, she'd come in from the garage, covered in dust, excited about her latest project and brimming with positive energy. My mom sculpted in marble and alabaster and sometimes concrete, and at one point we had a very impressive, six-foot-high Henry Moore–style piece on our front lawn. My mom's sculptures were mostly of the human form, not dark and edgy, like some of her paintings. My dad claimed he didn't have an artistic bone in his body, but he loved Mom's art because it made her happy.

Eventually, our family settled in Lorne Park, an established residential community in Mississauga. It was a great place to grow up: my siblings and I played on the swings in the schoolyard, rode our bikes, invented games and explored the ravine. My siblings and I usually made our own breakfasts, but my mom, who was a good cook, always prepared a nice dinner and otherwise looked after the house.

It was only when I was invited to dinner at my friends' that I began to realize my mom might not be like other mothers. And it wasn't just because she was artistic. For one thing, she talked to her mirror the way someone else might confide her innermost thoughts to a diary. She also talked to her ironing board. When she lacked props, she talked to herself.

My mom started each morning at her dressing table, where she twirled and pinned up her hair. Then she laid a towel on the floor and, clad in white bra and panties, did her exercises on it. During the week, she listened to classical music, but on Saturdays Daniele, Joerg and I would roll our eyes as polka folk music blasted from the radio. My mom was strong, and she had an innate knowledge of how to keep fit and trim. She did leg raises, push-ups, abdominal crunches, scissor kicks, bent-knee raises. Even while washing dishes, she would kick her legs out backwards and sideways.

Back at her dressing table, my mom applied a face mask, followed by her makeup, all the while talking to her mirror, completely in her own world. Sometimes she was positive—"Oh, what a beautiful day!"—but sometimes her monologues could whip into a frenzy of anger and regret: "Goddammit," she'd say, "I'm going to have to leave this family. I have so many talents I'm wasting with these kids tying me down."

I felt afraid whenever my mom talked like that, because sometimes it escalated into her screaming and then throwing things. She often mocked Daniele, declaring her to be stupid and dowdy and big and clumsy. Sometimes my mom would cry hysterically, saying that we had stolen her life from her, preventing her from becoming who she might have been in the world. Her outbursts brought out my steely will, so that I didn't feel sorry for her, not for a second.

My mom's beauty ritual took hours, during which we weren't allowed to disturb her. In fact, we were never allowed to interrupt her except at the right time—but when was that? Keeping pace with my mom's moods was an exhausting but essential life skill for all of us. Getting it wrong meant a lot of yelling, sighing and rolling of eyes. Catching her attention was like trying to grab a cobra by the tail.

My mom wanted to blame someone for her unhappiness. She would accuse me of stealing our dad's attention and of manipulating him to get something I wanted. Many nights I lay awake listening to her hollering, howling and smashing plates. Sometimes she would sob so hysterically and painfully that it made me sick to my stomach. I was afraid. I was angry. Mostly I just wanted to get the hell out of the house so that the noise would stop. Sometimes she was fighting with my dad, and sometimes she was just venting. It occurred often enough that I always went to bed with the fear that something bad might happen. Though I wanted to close my door, I left it open so I could keep watch over my little brother's room—I wanted to be able to hear if he was crying so that I could comfort him.

I remember one night when the screaming was so loud that the police were called. Two officers came to the house and separated us from our parents while they asked a ton of questions. I remember that it felt very serious and I was scared. So many of these traumatic incidents float around in my brain as if part of a nightmare.

Celebrations such as Christmas Eve, when we opened our gifts, would be wonderful—till my mom's stress level soared too high and the plates would start flying. Or I would be decorating pumpkins with my mom, excited by her irrepressible energy as she transformed our backyard into the spookiest in the neighbourhood, then find myself cowering in the kitchen that same evening as she once again smashed plates in a rage, the origin of which I couldn't imagine. One summer evening when I was eight, my mom became so angry with me for being sulky while we were eating outside that she smashed a stack of plates over my head, leaving me more shocked than hurt. That same summer I had such severe stomach pains from anxiety that I could barely eat. One climactic night, my mom smashed all the plates in the house, bundled up her three kids, then kicked through the glass front door and raced us through the streets in the car. When a policeman pulled us over, he asked her to get out of the car and noticed my mom's cut and bleeding foot. He gallantly and gently applied first aid. I was frustrated and scared—I wanted the officer to take care of my sister and brother and me, but as usual, it was my glamorous and charming mother who received the sympathetic attention.

My mom smacked me many times while simultaneously pummelling me with her words. Her attacks left me convinced that I was a devious, bad person. Her special weapon was a wooden spoon, but the scariest part of her attacks was their randomness. Since her rules felt arbitrary, she was always catching us off guard. If I dared say something to her that was unpleasant but true, she would give me a puppy-dog expression of *I am so hurt.* If I didn't back down, she would tell me how mean and selfish and ridiculous I was, then taunt me about my hairstyle, or my friends, or my teachers—anything she knew I was sensitive about—until I was in tears. Then she would either become sympathetic or accuse me of being hysterical. I had nowhere to turn to legitimize my feelings, and no one to tell me this wasn't okay.

When I was ten, Daniele was given permission to ride the city bus to the mall with a friend. Desperately wanting to go with her, I made a huge fuss about how unfair it was to have to stay behind. After shouting at me to smarten up, my mom dragged me inside, then beat me with a boot. I was crying and she was screaming. I don't remember how badly it hurt, but I do remember the shame I felt about my behaviour, and how afraid I was that my sister was now old enough to leave the house on her own—she was becoming independent and I was left behind. When Daniele was gone, my mom's focus was on me—and I didn't want any more of her negative attention.

My brother, Joerg, was a cute, mischievous kid who could do no wrong in my parents' eyes—at least when he was little. My mom used to take him in her arms, stroke his hair and call him her little *liebchen*, but I came to believe his upbringing might have been the most confusing of all, caught as he was between my mom's mercurial moods and my dad's great expectations. When Joerg was eight, he started sleeping with a knife under his pillow. He never needed to use it, but it lay close as he slept. Years later when I asked him why, he said, "I didn't trust Mom."

★　★　★

Like many stay-at-home mothers of her generation, my mom would often pour a late-afternoon cocktail. But when my mom was drinking, her personality changed. She would sometimes invite me to sit beside her on the couch, where she was reading and listening to music. She'd say, "I'm having such a lovely time. Come sit with me," and pat the couch beside her. If I sat down, she would stroke my hair, causing me to cringe because by then I hated her touch. My parents rarely talked about the war, but on these occasions she would tell sad stories of being a little girl and feeling so lost, and how her house was bombed during her tenth birthday party, leaving bodies lying on the street. She would talk about being half-starved and living in a single-bedroom apartment with her little sister and mother. She would tell me that she saw children whom she had babysat dead in their mothers' arms. She would describe the Russians taking over the city when the war ended, and being marched through the streets in the cold, and women being raped and her neighbourhood pillaged. I didn't know how to feel. The stories she told were horrifying, but this side of her was so unlike the part of her that lashed out. I was never sure which of her stories was real. If I pulled away, she would grow angry. "What's the matter with you?" she'd say. "You don't know how good you have it. *I* never had nice clothes!"

Some nights I could hear Joerg crying himself to sleep. Even though I was only ten, he was six and I felt like I needed to protect him. At times, I tiptoed in to ask if he was all right, and occasionally I would crawl into bed with him until he fell asleep, but I didn't know how to help him, as it was never just one thing in our house. We were too young, too inexperienced, to be able to put a finger on any specific event and say, "This is wrong."

By the time Joerg was ten, my sister and I were so immersed in sports that we were barely at home, leaving him alone. He found his own retreat. He would disappear down into the basement to spend hours watching television. I knew he was sad, but his endless TV watching drove me crazy. One evening when I wanted to read quietly downstairs after a track practice, my brother sat with the TV clicker behind his back, stubbornly refusing to turn off the set. He wanted to push my buttons and succeeded. As he laughed, I wound up and punched him in the shoulder—only to feel daggers of pain shoot up my baby finger. He only laughed harder as I swore at the pain.

My finger was broken, requiring a splint and adding another injury to the stress fractures I already had in both legs from running. The doctor showed me how to punch with my fingers tucked neatly inside my fist, but I never wanted to hit Joerg again.

I believe my mom loved us in her own way, but in her darkest hours, she would say things like "I could kill you and then kill myself." What seemed to transform her words into a frightening possibility was the fact that a distraught mother in a nearby neighbourhood had shot her kids, then herself. Another mother had gassed her family while they were sleeping. My mom would get worked into a frenzy—screaming and sobbing and throwing dishes. She would howl that she was going to gas us all. Her threat was that she would kill herself and take us with her. She never did anything to show that she'd go through with it, but I slept with my window open.

My mom later insisted her threats hadn't been serious, yet I felt that we lived in an unsafe house. It's hard to convey just how volatile the situation felt. I remember one day when my father was out trimming the hedges. There was a woman sun-tanning in a bikini in the yard next door, and my mother was consumed by jealousy—she felt my dad was staring. To punish him, she went into the basement and pulled out the plug from his power cord so that my dad would have to head down to the basement and plug it in again. This was repeated a few times before my father raced to catch my mother on her way into the basement and lock her in there. Up to this point it was almost silly—the plotline for an episode of *I Love Lucy*—but my mom's rage bubbled over. She grabbed an axe from the basement and hacked her way out through the door. For me, every day felt like it could take that kind of unpredictably scary turn. Perhaps Daniele and Joerg felt the same way, as we schemed together about an escape, for which we created a kit with bandages and a flashlight. We also saved getaway cash and planned whose doorstep we would land on if we needed to make a run for it.

As an adult, I have reflected with some humour on the misguided package Daniele and I put together, but I still feel our runaway plan should not be mistaken for the angry packing of a suitcase by children who suddenly hate their parents for shutting off the television set. In my mind, our motivation was survival.

I did have one best buddy who comforted me throughout my childhood: Bimbo, my white Maltese terrier with the huge underbite—twenty pounds of energy and toughness, and the smartest dog in the world. He ran free throughout the neighbourhood and was probably responsible for many litters of Maltese mutts. I admired his boldness, and I told him all my secrets, knowing he would never betray me.

My mom bought Bimbo for five dollars from a little boy who was selling three puppies outside the grocery store. One sunny afternoon when I was seven, he landed in my lap. Bimbo was officially a birthday present for Joerg, but I always considered him mine. Bimbo's name was the unfortunate result of my mom's not-quite-perfect English. While watching Bimbo the Clown on television with us, my mom would sing, "Bimbo, Bimbo, Bimbo!" in her high musical voice. The puppy lifted his ears and wagged his tail, sealing his fate.

Bimbo remains an enduring childhood memory. His misadventures were legendary not only in our family but also in our neighbourhood. Bimbo was the dog who allowed me to dress him in doll clothes, then wheel him around the neighbourhood in a carriage, until he finally became fed up and leapt free, still wearing diapers and a baby bonnet. Bimbo was the dog who regularly took on the 170-pound St. Bernard next door, tormented the Irish setter across the street and attacked any unleashed animal that ventured within ten feet of us. He was also the dog who followed me to school each day, so persistently escaping our home and sneaking into the school that the teacher finally allowed him to sleep at my feet. I became the girl with the funny dog, and when I began to run as a sport, Bimbo became my partner. I would put on my running shoes like Dorothy her red slippers, and together we would run up the yellow brick road.

Best of all, Bimbo was the smelly, wonderful, half-blooded prince, the most loyal and sensitive animal I would ever know.

He licked away my tears as I held him, sobbing at night, then wagged his tail when I stopped crying. He heard every word of hatred that I secretly flung at my mom. He heard my silent screams of anger as I struggled to hold myself together in an angst-filled world that made no sense. I've never forgotten my debt to Bimbo. Dogs have always played a big role in my life, and today my partner and I have two.

I had other friends in whom I could confide without fear—my stuffed animals, especially Bear-Bear, who was about two feet tall with a plush coat, felt paws, a head that turned and a mechanism that enabled him to make a low growling sound. While Bimbo had a life of his own, Bear-Bear was rock solid. I always made him *grrrr* at least twenty times before going to sleep. Surprisingly, Bear-Bear managed to survive my child-hood. Decades later, my kids used to have him in bed with them, though by then he'd lost his growl.

* * *

A few years ago, a former teacher sent me a letter after hearing me speak at the Living Arts Centre of Mississauga. "It's hard to imagine your transformation," the letter began, then went on to describe a little girl who came to art camp each day dressed in a white lacy dress, with bows in her flaxen hair—silent, shy and withdrawn.

Just like this teacher, I remember that child with the long white-blonde hair and bright blue eyes who took up so much space with her constantly moving Marmaduke limbs, who would jump at loud sounds and who would never raise her hand. She was the little girl who woke up crying in terror one night because she had forgotten to put her chair up on her desk and she feared that her grade-two teacher would give her the strap.

Yes, I remember that high-strung little girl, so impossibly visible, so impossibly silent.

By the time I started grade one, I had internalized so much guilt and shame from my mom's raw judgments of me, and from the ugly way my answering hatred made me feel, that I believed something was terribly wrong with me. I was a bad person, and anyone who came too close would see my evil and perhaps be hurt by it. I was afraid of all the social relationships I had to navigate at school—afraid of the other kids, who didn't like me because I was different; afraid of authority because I might get into trouble at any time, just like at home. I remember feeling wrapped in a veil of confusion, making it difficult to think straight.

I now love to read, yet I initially had trouble combining different letters of the alphabet to make sounds and words. By grade three, I was reading "cat" and "mat" but not understanding sentences. That summer my teacher, Jessie Finlayson, visited my house to explain to me that I had failed grade three, which I knew was an unusual thing to do. She brought a box of chocolates and told me what a great person I was. She explained that if I repeated grade three, school would become easier for me, and that I would do well from then on. She was so kind that it took away some of the humiliation of my having failed the year. By grade four, I was able to read, but math was—and still is—a great mystery to me. I was receiving a lot of extra help from my teachers, and I think one of the principals realized that something might be amiss. I was pulled out of class for what I now think was an assessment for learning disabilities, but the nice men and women with flash cards would also ask questions about my life at home. My mom sat in on this testing with me, but she didn't like anyone asking too many questions about our family. I'm not entirely sure what happened, but very soon after those evaluations I was moved to a new school. All of this left me unsteady. I wasn't the only kid struggling in class, but I definitely trailed the pack, leaving me with the feeling that I was not only a bad person but also a stupid one.

I wasn't picked on by the other kids, just left alone.

From time to time, I did have close friends. My mom could be charming to them, but she could also be scathing. She would tell one, for example, that she didn't like her blouse or how she wore her hair. Worse, she'd criticize a girl's parents to her face, then continue to air her views after the girl had left, scoffing about her mother's lack of style, about how she knew "that type of woman" and about how she was sure the girl's parents were trapped in a loveless marriage. Since having friends over typically meant subjecting them to scorn, I found it was easier to go to their houses.

No one with whom my mom came in contact was safe from her mean remarks, as predictable and memorable as they were inappropriate. She would tell the checkout girl at the grocery store, "You shouldn't wear that colour. It looks awful on you." If someone remarked in her presence, "Oh, I love that music!" she might roll her eyes with disdain. When we went to a restaurant, we'd have to move three times before my mom found just the right table. She would comment charmingly on the maître d's manners, then minutes later tell the waitress, "You know, that lipstick doesn't suit you at all." People seldom knew what to do with my mom's comments, because they were usually delivered in a fluty tone with a flirtatious batting of the eyelashes. But behind those lashes were my mom's cold, hard green eyes. And she could cut a person to shreds while wearing a lovely smile.

My mom's offensive remarks also alienated potential friends to whom my dad introduced her. It became easier for him to socialize on his own through golf or tennis, but this only exacerbated the problem, leaving her more isolated than ever.

Like many immigrants, my mom was especially isolated because she had left all her family behind in East Germany. Oma, her mother, visited us in 1977, when my parents flew her to Canada for a three-week holiday. The wall was still up, but according to my dad, the Communists had stopped caring whether older people left East Germany, as they were considered a drain on the economy. They could be granted special permission to visit relatives in West Berlin, and that was what Oma got. Then she boarded a plane to Toronto. Even though this was illegal, the East German government lacked computerized equipment to check on everyone, so a flight could be managed.

Oma looked exactly like you would picture an aging Frau—a big woman, standing foursquare in a housedress; beige pressure stockings over thick, strong legs; large breasts and a potbelly; her hair rolled over her ears. Despite her scary appearance, she had a soft heart. She paid attention to us kids, and I liked her.

Oma was overwhelmed by our grocery stores, the bins

piled high with fruits and vegetables, for which we didn't have to line up. When one of us touched the produce, she gasped in protest, "Don't do that!" We had to explain, "But that's how you put what you want in the bag." I remember her eating an entire pineapple. She had never tasted one before, and she couldn't believe its sweetness. Even when her mouth became sore from the acid, she still wanted more.

Oma and my mom had one big, fabulous fight while she was visiting. I don't know what it was about, and now that I have children of my own, I understand those types of explosions. Back then, though, I wanted to know why my mom was screaming at Oma. I wanted to know what had made her so angry. I wanted to know the truth of my mom's life in Germany. My oma didn't speak English, and I didn't speak a lot of German. She said, "Your mom has always been difficult, but it wasn't her fault." I had no idea what she meant. I could only think back to the harshness of the postwar stories my mom had told me and wonder how that might have affected young Seigrid.

After that visit, Oma disappeared from our lives. When the wall came down in 1989, I was eager for news of her, thinking that without the political barrier we might be able to reach her. When I questioned my mom, she told me that she hadn't been able to make contact.

I recently reconnected with my mom's family. I know now that my oma lived until 1997, so it would have been possible to visit her. Now I wish that I had kept asking questions and pushing, but my mom shut down this conversation by remarking, "Why focus on things that are sad?" I yearned then, as now, to learn more about my mom, including what bitterness may have passed between her and my oma.

Perhaps if I had more information about my mom's early life, I would be better able to understand her, or at least be more empathetic. I would understand her need to suck up all the oxygen in any room she entered, and her inability ever to blend into the background. I would comprehend why she always insisted on wearing something eye-catching that would make her the star—never for her the grey wool dress. During my teen years, I lived in constant fear of my friends, teachers and especially my enemies coming in contact with my mom. Whenever her eccentricities were on display, I would explain, "Well, you know, she's an artist." I continued using that excuse as an adult when friends wondered why I didn't see more of my mom. I felt guilty, but not guilty enough to invite her for a visit, with all its hazards.

One of the things about my mom that I still appreciate is the importance she placed on exercise, on enjoying nature, on breathing fresh air and staying physically active. As a family, we liked to eat dinner in our backyard and to go on picnics. On Sundays, we took long walks. No matter how young we were or what the temperature, my mom always made sure my siblings and I went outside for part of each day. When I was in grade two, I was home sick for over a month with pneumonia. Although it was November, my mom figured I needed fresh air to clear my lungs, so she bundled me in a sleeping bag and plopped me outside on a lawn chair. Whether this helped, or how a doctor might view this treatment, I have no idea, but it lifted my spirits to feel the winter sun on my face and to shake off the disorientation that comes with a lengthy illness. To this day, I don't feel I've lived properly until I've spent part of every twenty-four hours outside. After a couple of days at a conference, I become insanely determined to escape. Sometimes I awaken at 4:30 in the morning for a power walk through snowstorms and torrential rains. In Ottawa, I've jogged in -28°C weather, my lungs protected by a scarf. When I'm dying, I hope someone will wheel me outside so I can turn my face toward the sun and just breathe.

It was through sports that I began to stand out in a positive way and to feel I belonged to a group. Though it wasn't the A group, this provided me with a comfort zone. From grades six to eight, when I attended Tecumseh Public School, I surprised myself by winning almost everything on Track and Field Day. I was skinny with long legs, and I could fly past even the boys. In grade six, a gym teacher started a track club; the aim was to run a hundred miles in three months. I ran a lot more than that, so I won a badge, which was presented to me in front of the whole school. It was a proud moment—and I wasn't used to feeling proud of myself. It felt great—and I somehow understood that sports were a way to make me feel this good again.

Of course, whenever my sister and I won a trophy, our mom had to claim the honour as her own. In our house, there was never any room for anybody else's problems, pains, joys or successes; my mom had the market covered. Show her a blue ribbon for track and she would exclaim, "Oh yes, I was quite a runner in school. I could also do the long jump." After we began to win Olympic medals, she was sure she could have been an Olympian if only her kids hadn't held her back.

When I was in public school, physical education became more integrated into the curriculum, so that excelling at it provided a much stronger sense of *wow!* In grade eight, my big goal was to win a Canada Fitness Award of Excellence. I'd worked hard and progressively, but I still hadn't conquered the dreaded flexed-arm hang, requiring me to grab a bar with both hands, pull up my body until my eyes were level with the bar, then hold that position for at least ninety excruciating seconds. Again and again I'd fall unceremoniously to the floor after forty seconds of agony. By test day, I still hadn't broken the one-minute barrier, and I had butterflies all morning waiting for the tryout.

After my classmates and I had suited up in our red T-shirts and blue polyester shorts, we took our stations along the bar. For the first thirty seconds, my flexed hang felt effortless. By the next fifteen, I had begun to shake. After a minute, I was shaking so hard I could feel the bar vibrate. By then, all the other kids had dropped off and I was alone on the increasingly shaky apparatus. I wouldn't give up. With thirty seconds to go, the whole bar was visibly moving because of the tremors running through my body, and I knew that my face had turned bright red. When the teacher yelled, "Ninety!" I simply opened my hands and fell to the ground, arms still flexed.

After I recovered, I turned around to find the entire class watching me. That was flattering, albeit a little embarrassing.

During my final public-school assembly, I was to receive not only the Canada Fitness Award of Excellence but also an academic award for most improved student.

The teacher called my name, and in the moment before I walked onto the stage, it happened. A shrill, high-pitched yell pierced the air: "Oh, Silken!"

The audience grew silent, then burst out laughing. I stood

on stage, a painfully self-conscious fourteen-year-old, absolutely mortified.

Later that afternoon, at the school's graduation party, someone must have signalled as I entered the room. Twenty-odd voices yelled, "Oh, Silken!"

*　*　*

Now, with some distance, I can cite many qualities in my mom that I admire: her energy, her creativity, her intelligence, her dynamism, her confident sense of herself as a woman. I can understand how she was shaped by her frightening past, and I can feel empathy for some of her insecurities and frustrations. I also know that the feelings of danger and distrust she bred in me fuelled an intense desire for independence and for the kind of achievement that would provide me with the security I did not have at home. I could not have raced, endured and won at Barcelona without that drive, or without an ability to deny and override pain.

Despite such triumphs, I know that some of my early wounds still bleed or cause warps in my personality. I know it's necessary for me to acknowledge this, and to let myself feel this old pain as part of my healing.

The toughest, most damaging, most enduring myth about our family was that it was "normal"—but I knew that our "normal" didn't feel *right*. And so it was deeply confusing that my siblings and I were never allowed to believe anything was wrong. After a while, even if you don't stop believing something is wrong, you *do* accept that you can't change it. My family clung to "normal" as if it were a life raft, yet I was still drowning, drowning in the confusion, drowning in endless anxiety, drowning in a loneliness that would last most of my life.

Even today I feel the stress of those old prohibitions. I still fear breaking the lock on our family's dark secrets. What I fear even more is not doing so.

MY DAD

Nineteen-year-old Hans Laumann had passed by the Canadian consulate in Hamburg many times before that day in 1955 when he impulsively walked through the door and applied to immigrate.

When I asked what gave him the courage, he replied, "I wanted to get as far away as possible from my old man."

My dad was born in 1936 in Hammer, a small town north of Hamburg, the second oldest in a family of three boys and one girl: Werner, Hans, Rolf and Etta—Etta being the second youngest. His father, Hans Bernhardt Laumann, was a first-class cabinetmaker but a terrible businessman. He could have made a decent living for his family if he hadn't disdainfully turned down work that didn't flatter his talents. When each of his sons reached age eight, Hans began to rush them through their schoolwork so they could labour in his shop, sometimes until midnight, preparing the wood and working the heavy machinery.

Opa was a nasty taskmaster who took out his mean temper on his family. He did not hesitate to beat his sons, and to intimidate them with his gruff, authoritative manner. He was even harsher on the women of his family. His wife cowered when he raised his voice; he hurled insults at her daily, and my dad suspected that he beat her as well. Opa guarded his only daughter, Etta, like property, and once when she came home late and he suspected she had a boyfriend, he chained her to a chair.

Oma was afraid of her husband, with good reason. When I was eleven, Daniele and I visited them in Hammer. I remember Oma sitting on the couch after preparing a three-course lunch, eyes glazed in exhaustion. She loved her grandchildren and was sweet-natured with us, but when her husband spoke to her, she cringed, and when he commanded, she jumped. I was too young then to understand the family dynamic—that Oma was severely abused, physically, mentally and emotionally, along with the four children. My dad had a difficult relationship with his father but adored his mother. Oma had Parkinson's disease, partly explaining her shaky hands and vacant look, which I noticed when she dared to sit down to relax. Dad usually speaks matter-of-factly about his dad; his voice is tinged with bitterness when he talks about his mother's suffering. She died before her husband.

My dad came to Canada by boat with no money in his pockets but his head full of dreams for creating a better life. He was not afraid of hard work, and so, while staying with a family friend for the first few months, he immediately began earning what he could in any way possible. After he had used his entrepreneurial skills to create Sparkle Window Cleaning, he brought both of his brothers from Germany, and for a time they all worked in the business. His younger brother, Rolf, is still a partner, but his older brother, Werner, dropped out to establish his own cabinetmaking business. My younger brother Joerg has just recently taken over the business.

My dad worked each weekday from 6 a.m. till 6 p.m., when our family would sit down for dinner together. On Saturdays, he cleaned windows, provided on-site estimates or caught up on his office work, while the kids stamped invoices, sorted mail or handed out flyers. That allowed us to spend more time with him while giving our mother a break. I looked forward to our adventures at the Sparkle office because it made me feel included in my dad's world and important enough to be helping.

Like Mom, my dad was driven to improve himself. After he had built up the business enough to buy us a home in Lorne Park, he went to night school to earn a degree in hopes of becoming a lawyer. It was a gruelling regimen, and one day he collapsed behind the wheel of his car. That's when he decided he didn't want to put his family through the sacrifices necessary for him to fulfill his dream—though he always held on to the idea that he would have made a great lawyer. I've never doubted his intelligence, and I sometimes wonder if my sister's decision to become a lawyer was, at least unconsciously, her completion of our father's dream.

Thanks to Dad's hard work and sacrifices, our family enjoyed a good, solid middle-class life. Some of my most delightful memories are of holidays at our beautiful Georgian Bay cottage, which smelled of cedar. For one special road trip, the summer before I turned twelve, my dad loaded my sister, my brother, Bimbo and me into his silver Volvo sedan, which was prone to overheating, and drove us across North America. Sometimes we camped; sometimes we stayed in hotels. It was perfect, except for the panicky time when we realized we'd left Bimbo at the last gas station. We found him, patiently waiting, tail wagging.

My dad gave me and my siblings love in the way a father gives love, but also in the way a mother gives love. He was much more affectionate than most of my friends' fathers, and far more connected to what we were doing. He was the one who drove us to our various lessons, who helped us with our homework and who became involved in our sports. He poured everything he had into raising us, including enthusiastically supporting our dreams.

From the moment my legs could move fast enough, running became a huge part of my life, and my dad was a huge part of that. Just like me, he's simultaneously athletic and clumsy. It's as if parts of our bodies grew too fast. Coordination takes time for us to master, while our tenacity and big lungs allow us to excel at repetitive sports like running, cycling and rowing. My dad ran for fitness, and eventually he invited me to join him. I loved it. I would put on my running shoes and fly all over Mississauga. Running meant release from a life in which I felt trapped. It spelled freedom. When I began to excel at it, it compensated for the struggles I was having with my schoolwork. It taught me that I had the power, through sport, to change my life in a significant way.

In grade eight, I was the best runner at Tecumseh Public School, which gave me the confidence to believe I might be able to join the Mississauga Track and Field Club. My dad made the call to the club the summer I graduated elementary public school, and all week I vibrated with nervousness, wondering how I'd do at my Thursday-evening tryout. After a three-kilometre warm-up, during which I had to push hard to keep up with the rest of the group, the middle-distance coach asked me to do an 800-metre timed run. I did it in around 2.35, which isn't very fast, but he decided I was good enough to join the club, and for the next couple of years, track dominated my life.

We met for a six-to-nine practice at least three evenings a week, and on Sundays we did the big run, anywhere from 12 to 16 kilometres around the 2.5-kilometre loop. Since my dad drove me to practice, he figured he might as well do the workout too. He was a great running partner, always encouraging, never impatient when I got a cramp or complained about how tired I was. Despite being in his forties, he could pull a 10-kilometre run without a problem, sometimes after a full day's work—he would just relax for twenty minutes and then be ready to go. Usually parents in their forties are too slow to pace their kids. My dad was so athletic, and had such a strong ability to push himself, that even at the end of a long workout he would challenge me to race the last 500 metres, and man, would we ever go, trying to beat each other. Once I started to train seriously, my dad would never let me win, partly because he wanted me to exert myself to the fullest, and partly because he's so competitive I doubt he could throw a race even if he wanted. I was fourteen before I could beat him. That happened for the first time in a 15-kilometre race at the Bread and Honey Festival in Streetsville. It meant a great deal to me, and I think my dad was also excited when I achieved that milestone.

During the week, if the weather was cold or windy, my sister sometimes ran with me. By this time, she was already training for rowing. I was a better runner than Daniele because

I was younger and lighter, but she had great endurance and was always game for a workout. We would run, side by side, for 10, 12, 16 kilometres, but during the last kilometre I would pick up the pace until I was sprinting—I just couldn't stop myself. Daniele sometimes took the bait, but more often she'd wave me on ahead, knowing that I needed to win more than she did.

At the track club, I could keep up with some of the middle-packers, but given my height (five foot ten) and muscular frame, no one expected me to be a distance runner. After our team workouts, all of us would take off our shoes and do strides on the grass, which was how I became friends with the other runners. Everyone was so nice, and because we spent so much time together, I felt for the first time that I had a social group. Being one of the youngest meant I was attending parties with kids in their late teens, but we didn't get into much trouble beyond a bit of drinking, as we were all too busy training and racing.

Now that I am older, I'm even more aware of what "average" looks like in an adult, causing me to marvel anew at my dad's athletic ability at forty, then fifty, then sixty and now at seventy-six. Five years ago, he did a 10-kilometre memorial run for a friend without stopping, having not practised for over a year. Then, three years ago, he competed in a two-day, 320-kilometre bike race, winging it with his buddies, who had been training, and even managing to beat them in the sprint. Along with a ton of natural ability, my dad is tough. He doesn't let physical pain become a barrier between him and finishing a race. His muscles could be cramping and he could be exhausted, but he's going to make it over the finish line. In energy and ability, he runs laps around his peers—a trait I see in Daniele and myself. Both of us can push ourselves all day, then still have enough left for an evening's workout. It's obvious that we've inherited our dad's mental and physical tenacity, giving us another reason to be grateful to him.

As well as being energetic, Dad has always been an exceptionally likable, generous and fun-loving guy with no pretensions. Whether someone is royalty or a labourer, he treats them the same. He's also delightfully spontaneous. If he is on his way to dinner and he spots a kid with a soccer ball, he just might roll up his dress pants and kick the ball around with the kid for a while. He likes to golf in his bare feet because it feels good. We'd be having dinner and a cherry would fly past one of our ears. One April Fool's Day, he convinced me and Daniele and Joerg that horseradish scooped with a melon-ball server was ice cream.

Dad never let self-consciousness get in the way of having a good time. When my sister and I were in high school, we decided to have a reverse-role party, where the guys dressed as girls and vice versa. My dad turned up in a purple velvet dress and had a wonderful time. He loved to dance, despite his terrible sense of rhythm.

The most conspicuous way in which my dad's brutal home life growing up surfaced in our family was in his temper, which sometimes made living with him difficult. Occasionally a very small offence would cause him to blow up. One day when I was eight, I left my new coat on the grass, where I'd been playing in the leaves. Dad dragged me out of the house by the ear, shoved me down onto the coat and demanded,

"Does this new coat belong on the grass?" He wasn't violent, but I worried that I might accidentally set him off.

The legacy of war had a huge impact on my parents. Looking only on the bright side was a coping tool for them in the struggle to build a good life in a new country without money, without family, without fluency. When I was old enough to know our mother's behaviour was not normal, my father continued to downplay her actions and their effects on us. The abuse, violence and deprivation that both he and Seigrid had lived through during World War II became his yardstick for measuring everything that went on in our family: *Don't you have plenty of food? Don't you have nice clothes? Aren't you safe from danger?*

Many of my first-generation Canadian friends have similar stories of parents whose strong work ethic, frugality and optimism allowed them to repress the pain of their past, including all thoughts of what they had lost. They were tough masters at stuffing down negativity and moving on. They didn't have time to work through their heavy baggage because they needed every drop of physical and mental energy to build a better future for their children.

My dad had a powerful vision of the privileged life he and Mom had provided us through perseverance and sacrifice, and we risked his anger if we challenged that. Everyone in our family espoused as gospel—at least on the surface, which was part of my childhood confusion—the view "Yes, we had some hard times, but it wasn't so bad." All those nights when I stayed awake to my mom's screaming and the crashing of dishes *weren't so bad.* My mom's belittling comments *weren't so bad.* Bottling up all those negative experiences to comply with the family script did as much damage to me as the initial pain because the negation of my reality made me crazy all over again.

I know that neither Dad nor Mom ever meant to hurt us. My siblings and I were the product of a harsh and complex backstory that all three of us have refused to pass down to another generation. I do not know the details of my parents' journeys. I only know my own. I also know that if we don't heal the past, it weaves its way into our present and controls us in ways that we don't even realize. In my family life, I never felt like I had worth. For me, achieving—becoming a champion—felt like the only way I could prove to myself that I was worth it, that I was a person of value. But the medals didn't free me—only confronting the truth could.

In my quiet moments I was still Silken, and if I couldn't love and honour myself, my inner life would remain a living hell.

MY BODY

Though things were difficult at home, sports had become my escape. I'd fallen in love with running with my dad, and as I grew into a teenager, it became a bigger and bigger part of my life. Unlike many young girls, I actually liked my body. It was strong and it was fast. It helped me win, and winning made me feel special—something I didn't often feel at home or in class. But when I got my period at eleven, all of that started to shift. All of a sudden, my body was changing not just in response to training but also in other ways—ways I didn't want it to. I was extremely self-conscious—even the slightest trace of fat on my thighs meant that I was starting to develop hips and breasts, something that scared me because it meant I was becoming a woman, and so was one step closer to becoming like my mom. For years she had obsessed over her figure, and when Daniele started to develop curves, my mom would suggest that Daniele was eating too much and call her clumsy and big. I wanted to do everything I could to prevent my body from developing, so I threw myself even more into my workouts and started to think very carefully about what I ate. I'd always been the kind of kid who would clear the refrigerator because I was so active. I would eat eight pieces of toast loaded with butter and jam for breakfast, and three bowls of cereal after practice as a pre-dinner snack. I'd never gained an ounce. But now I was petrified that all of that would change, so I monitored my food very closely, hoping to delay the inevitable.

When I hit the road in my sneakers, I found a haven. I was alone with my thoughts and felt in control of my world. But when I was fourteen, I had two experiences in close succession that shook those feelings of safety. First, an older boy I trusted—a teammate of mine—suddenly pulled me into the bushes during a run, forcing himself on top of me and kissing me. I shoved him off, but his approach left me rattled—what on earth had I done to make him think I wanted that? The second was a much more serious encounter—one that even now gives me chills. I set out one day for my normal run, a ten-kilometre route that took me through my neighbourhood and down to a more isolated trail along the lakeshore in Mississauga. As I moved along the trail, a man pulled up and got out of his car. He started to jog after me, saying that he wanted to run with me—would I run with him? I picked up my pace and headed back to my neighbourhood as quickly as possible. There was something about him that scared me. He followed me in his car, talking to me through the open window as my eyes scanned the streets for help. Finally, I spotted a house with Block Parent sign in the window. I was too embarrassed to knock—I felt that I was probably overreacting—but I went behind the house and hid in the backyard for several minutes. When I returned to the street, the man was still there. I hid behind two more Block Parent houses, waiting for what felt like an impossibly long time, but each time I got back to the sidewalk, there he was. Desperate, I broke out in a sprint for home, and he chased me on foot, trying to convince me to go with him at first and then physically trying to pull me back to his car. I fought him off and bolted for my front door, shaking like a leaf. I remember clearly that my parents were both home when I stumbled in, but I didn't say a word to them. I have no idea why. I think I felt that I'd done something wrong to attract this man's attention. My shorts were too short. My ponytail was too flirtatious. The fault was somehow mine.

From that moment on, I withdrew even deeper into my body. I cut my hair and started restricting my calories to just eight hundred a day. I had to do whatever I could to get back to that place where my body was strong and fast and nothing more.

I confided in my best friend, Jane Vincent, not because I thought I had an eating disorder, but because I couldn't understand how I could be consuming so little and not lose weight. Jane did her best to convince me that I was already too skinny, though I believe it was Daniele who officially rang the alarm. My track club sent me with my dad to a clinic Mississauga, where I was diagnosed as anorexic. My condition was not yet life-threatening, but the team of nutritionists scared me into understanding that not eating was already undermining my schoolwork, my chance of being optimal in sports and my future ability to have children. Though I wasn't cured, I was jolted into becoming more aware of my body's normal needs, partly because I didn't want to create a situation requiring monitoring, but mostly because I wanted to run—and to win.

Daniele came to my rescue in another way, too. In the summer of 1982, after I'd been sidelined from running because of stress fractures in both legs, she persuaded me to join the Don Rowing Club. My intention was just to keep in condition for track; instead, I found myself becoming consumed, albeit without much skill but with a lot of heart. During midday naps, I would hit the wall with my hands as I dreamed that I was practising the strokes.

For my first race, I borrowed an old boat and finished in the top ten singles, which was considered exceptional. After I broke through the boat's foot stretcher, which was twenty years old and weakened by water damage, my dad bought my sister a new boat, costing about $5,000, and I inherited her old one.

I established at least one record that summer: for boat tipping, which forced me to become adept at climbing back in. This required me to hold both oars with one arm while raising my legs as high as the boat, which would be floating at waist level. Usually I flung my body over the bow, got my legs up onto the decking, then scooted myself onto my seat, still clutching the oars.

My talent for capsizing had a lot to do with my desire to put all of my body weight behind those oars, which meant hauling on my blades well before I had the skill to balance the boat by pulling them squarely through the water. I was also drawing on an inner intensity from some place below my level of consciousness. All I knew was that when my coach yelled "Go!" I pulled as hard and as long as I could with everything I had, often causing my stomach to cramp. This is the level of drive needed by Olympic athletes for a strenuous workout, but with me it was always there, so that even as a novice I pulled myself to exhaustion. It took many years for me to learn the benefits of knowing how to row light.

All that summer I clung to the illusion that I would return to running, while already knowing in my heart that I'd found my sport. I had also made friends with rowers who were on the National Team, or on the cusp of making it. Each morning, I biked three kilometres to the Don Rowing Club, then rowed fifteen kilometres before sun up. After school, I ran eight kilometres, then performed core-strengthening exercises before bedtime. Along with Daniele, Jane had steadfastly encouraged me to row. As young teenagers, I'm sure Jane and I irritated the older athletes with our giggling and general silliness, while making our own time at the boathouse much more fun. We found ourselves laughing hysterically at her wacky homemade shorts, the earnest tone of a coach, and the antics of another friend, Cary Harvey. Unfortunately, Jane found she was too short for success in the sport; she later competed as a cross-country skier in the 1988 Olympic Games in Calgary.

My short-term plan when I started rowing was to make the National Team in my first attempt. It was crazy and totally implausible, but I was determined. After I connected with Jack Nicholson, a National Team coach who knew my sister, he sent me a training program, which I followed to the letter. Ignorance was my secret weapon, because I had no idea how hard it would be to master this sport and how physically demanding. Everything about rowing is counterintuitive. If you feel unbalanced, the natural instinct is to panic and pull your oars, exactly the right way to tip the boat—too high, too low or letting go altogether. Another common error is to panic when you hit a wave and to let go of the oars. Both responses are a great way to learn to swim.

Rowing came just at the right moment in my life. It moved me from the running world, where I felt too big and too heavy, into a world where my height and naturally muscular build were just right. My kind of body was the ideal, and I think that helped to pull me away from my spiral into anorexia. But even though my body was right for rowing, I was far from totally making peace with it. Biceps were not yet considered desirable or sexy for a woman, and I remember how upset I was when a gym coach, who hadn't seen me since my weight had risen from 130 to 140 and then to 155 pounds, remarked in shock, "Wow, have you ever changed! You should watch what you're eating." The face was different, but what I heard was an echo of my mom's mocking words.

Like too many other woman, I came to equate control of my body with control over my life. I couldn't control my mom or my dad, or those who didn't like me, or my marks in math, but I *could* control what food I put in my mouth. Since my life felt so fragile and unsafe, the desire to be in charge in this one way became so paramount that sometimes it seemed like a life-and-death struggle. I was convinced that if I allowed my weight to get out of control, I would lose my grip on how my future would unfold.

* * *

It was while I was in high school that my mom moved out of the house. She returned for a few months, then left again. She'd been threatening to do this for so many years that I think I'd come to the point of "Well, leave already." I don't remember missing her. I think it was a relief to be free of all that drama and disruption, especially now that I was beginning to understand her toxic influence. After an earlier visit to our house, my friend Jane had said to me, "You shouldn't let your mother talk to you that way. I wanted to stop her, but I didn't have the words." I burst into tears, grateful not only for the sympathy but also for this belated corroboration of how I felt.

My mom rented a studio with another artist in a warehouse downtown, where I sometimes visited her. It felt odd and awkward, creaking upward in a rickety metal-cage elevator. We had enjoyed a suburban, middle-class existence, and now here she was living with exposed pipes and brick walls, probably in a space that was illegal. Because she had been disconnected from my life for so long, we didn't have much to talk about, but she seemed excited about living out her dream of becoming a professional artist.

My mom had talent, especially as a sculptor. She worked hard, she was passionate and some of her pieces were very beautiful. A few agents and potential patrons encouraged her work; she exhibited in various galleries, and she received a number of private commissions. However, just as her distrust had cast a veil of suspicion over our neighbours, my teachers and my friends' parents, so too did her emotional health start to dominate her professional life. When a wealthy businessman commissioned several large pieces, then offered to help her secure a spot with a major gallery, she became suspicious of his intentions rather than grateful for his interest. After creating two works in alabaster for him, she refused any more commissions.

After two years at Lorne Park, I switched to the Independent Education Centre, or INDEC, which was an alternative school for grades eleven to thirteen. Most of INDEC's other students had social problems, like being teenaged mothers; nevertheless, the school provided me with the flexibility I needed to train at the rowing club and to do my schoolwork on my own time. It also provided an unexpected bonus: it freed me from the boredom that had plagued my early school years. Then, I had watched the clock, waiting for the bell to ring so I could do the things that really excited me, like sports, reading, playing the piano, and hanging out with Jane and my rowing friends. At INDEC, the structure was similar to what I would experience at university, allowing me to meet with teachers one on one, attend lectures and work hard in short, compressed bursts instead of enduring idle time in the classroom.

Until then, I'd been an earnest student who stayed up late to study without a lot to show for it. INDEC unshackled my creative self. One male English teacher, who unabashedly wore makeup, took groups of us to downtown Toronto for Bertolt Brecht plays. I began reading all kinds of books, writing poetry and growing excited about how to use words to express my ideas.

By throwing myself so passionately into sports, I'd missed out on a whole part of teenage life by default, like going to proms, having my hair and makeup done, mooning over guys and shopping. At INDEC, I exchanged my prissy clothes for men's army pants, cut my hair short and wore safety pins in my ears. The style suited my dynamic new life and had the added advantage of driving my mom crazy.

Unfortunately, neither the success I achieved rowing nor my inspiring new academic life was enough to undo the

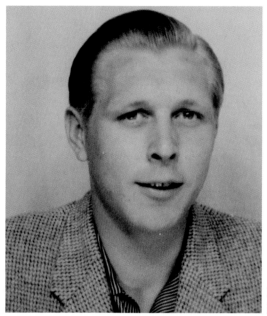

My handsome dad, Hans, in his early twenties.

My beautiful mother, Sigitta, with Daniele and me, 1966.

On a family trip back to Germany, 1976. My father's father, Bernhardt, my little brother, Joerg, me, my mom and Daniele standing in front of the Rheine.

My mother and Joerg, in 1977.

Posing with the bike my mother gave me on the first day of high school, 1980. I loved those red saddlebags, but they were a bit nerdy.

With my friend Jane Vincent at the Streetsville Bread and Honey race, June 1981. Running gave me a new sense of belonging, as well as an enthusiasm for sport that I would soon bring to rowing.

My coach Mike Spracklen and I having our pre-race talk at five a.m. before the San Diego World Cup, May 1990. The dour expression on my face is only from our early start to avoid rough water and the winds that morning—Mike always knew exactly the right thing to say to me.

The little red Honda Civic my boyfriend, John, and I packed up with our worldly possessions before moving to Victoria from our home in Toronto, to train with Mike. John drove the whole way because every time the car started down the highway I fell asleep! August 1990.

John was my constant support as I fought to come back from my injuries. Here we are just days before leaving for the Olympics, at the beautiful Victoria home of Marilyn and Peter Copland, July 1992.

Just strokes away from winning a bronze medal in Barcelona. The look of pain on my face is even worse than I remember, but I was determined not to quit. August 2, 1992.

This was snapped moments after I won the bronze medal. I was thrilled when I looked over the grandstand to see a sea of red and white, so many friends and family had come to Barcelona to support our team.

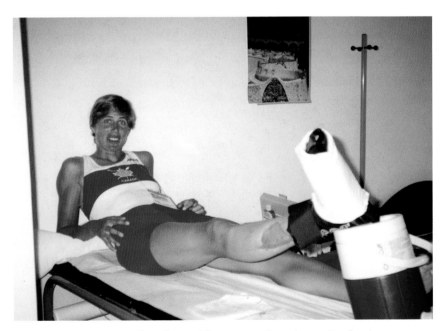

My sprint to recovery after the accident meant long hours in physio. Here I am icing my aching leg at the medical clinic, directly after the final in Barcelona.

KIM VAN BRUGGEN

John and I walk under a canopy of oars held by our Olympic team-mates on our wedding day, September 24, 1993.

BRENDA COLBY

After having walked me down the aisle, my dad shares some words of love.

With my mom after winning a Silver medal at the 1996 Summer Games in Atlanta. It was special to have her there at the final race of my career.

William, knapsack on his back, getting one last hug before his first day of school, with Kate behind me. Although we were separated at this point, John and I worked hard to keep things as normal as possible, and we took William to school together. September 2002.

Coming together with Patch and his girls for our first summer at Stoney Lake, in Ontario, in 2009. Clockwise from top right: Patch, Tygre, Kate, William and me.

Patch and I hiking through Mystic Beach on Vancouver Island in 2009, the year we spent getting to know each other before Patch moved to Victoria. Being active outdoors is one of our shared passions.

Kilee on a trip to a water park in 2011. While life with Kilee can sometimes be challenging, I revel in the joy she derives from our family outings.

On the rocks outside our home, Patch, Tygre, Kilee, Kate, William and I pose in a rare family photo together, 2013.

damage inflicted on my psyche as a child. I began to look for bigger outlets for my pain.

I was sixteen the first time I cut myself with a razor. It was a Friday night and I wanted to go out on a date. So did my dad. If we both went out, Joerg would be left home alone. My dad, Daniele and I had already been butting heads over my desire for independence. They thought I was being too bold, attending events in Toronto and sometimes coming home on the midnight GO train. Since I was focused on training for the Olympics and excelling at school, I didn't think I was being irresponsible, but this one night, it came to a head.

Furious that I was insisting on leaving, my dad demanded, "You can't leave Joerg alone all the time. You're being selfish."

I was angry, but my dad's approval was still desperately important to me, and I crumpled in shame. I did feel the need to take care of Joerg, and I worried that my wanting to leave made me a bad person. Everything was falling apart. My mom was gone, and my dad was out of the house a lot. The pressure on me felt unbearable. Shaking with conflicting emotions, I went out into the yard and sat under a tree with a razor blade I'd grabbed from the bathroom. I had been playing with this razor for quite some time; whenever self-doubt broke through my fragile facade of confidence, I'd fantasized about slitting a vein just to end my anguish and confusion and self-hate. I would put its edge to my wrist, and its sharpness would feel so good that I wanted to go deeper to release the pressure building inside me so hard and fast that I felt I might explode. Now, with anger boiling through me, I was both desperate enough and ready enough. I didn't want to slash my wrist in order to kill myself, nor did I want to injure myself so badly that I would have to go to a hospital—that part of my mind was still working. Instead, I cut lightly but deliberately and repeatedly to release some of my anguish so I could survive. It felt good to bleed, providing temporary relief. It also terrified me that I could do this to myself, and that someday I might possibly be tempted to go further.

Razors continued to attract me, and I would arrive at this place again a few more times after this episode. I'd toy with the razor, drawing it across my wrist in order to nick the skin. Even the thought of being able to do this served as a safety valve, making the pressure I felt more bearable. It became my secret, my private shame, never to be revealed to anyone.

It was yet another behaviour that punished my innocent, forgiving body without ever solving anything, just like my more pervasive eating disorder. It took decades before I understood that an eating disorder is a lifetime addiction, like alcoholism. Even as an adult, losing pounds to deal with unbearable stress has proven a hard habit for me to break. When my marriage ended, I dropped from a size ten to a size six in only a few months. Initially, I experienced a huge sense of release because it fed my illusion that everything was under control, and the more weight I lost, the more compliments I received, since my neurosis reflected our society's hang-up. My tailor took in my suits twice before announcing, in broken English, "You too skinny. Start eating."

Anorexia and cutting—like alcoholism—are self-abusive activities that deflect energy from addressing life's real challenges and disappointments head-on. There is tremendous shame in admitting to anorexia because it acknowledges the fear that lurks at the core of the disorder: *I am not in control.*

When my counsellor, Neil, pressed me, I smartly replied that I sometimes experienced "disordered eating" triggered by stress. That sounded far less dramatic than admitting I'm an anorexic. Fortunately, Neil had a way of cutting through all my clever attempts to hide the seriousness of my problem, helping me to bear witness, out loud, to the truth of what I was actually experiencing. *Disordered eating?* How about: *Loathing my body? Feeling guilty every time I eat? Flirting with the desire to sink into the pseudo-comfort of my obsession?*

Like any other addiction, anorexia takes hold of your brain and never fully lets go. At times, I still long to drop weight to prove I'm in control, while knowing in my deepest self that missing meals proves I'm *not* in control. Pulling away from this illness offered the same challenges as any other addiction, with this twist: I was trying to refrain from refusing myself, whereas most addicts are trying to abstain from indulging themselves.

I'm so grateful to my body for having its own intelligence and for being patient with me. Each day, I thank it for staying strong through decades of intermittent starvation, as well as the years I pushed it to extremes of performance and then through the pain of physical injury. Many anorexic women have not been able to bear children. They have destroyed their bone density, leading to multiple fractures, and exposed themselves to serious autoimmune diseases. Great genetics and the grace of God continue to keep me healthy and vibrant in spite of my years of self-loathing and abuse.

Like other women athletes, I have also been made self-conscious about my body because of a cultural bias pitting muscles against femininity. When a woman pulls on oars, or sprints, or jumps onto a bobsled, or hurls herself down a mountain, she develops muscles, often big ones seen as unattractive, perhaps even repulsive, by many people.

Including my mom.

I remember a winter's evening when she dared to wander down into the training pit that Daniele and I had created in our family's furnace room. After our run in the blistery weather, the two of us would do a circuit with fifty squats on the rickety rack that Daniele and my dad had made from two-by-fours, followed by two hundred bench pulls. When my mom approached, we were midway through a circuit. My face was red and sweaty; I had a huge pack of sand-filled Canadian Tire weights on my back, and Daniele was spotting me: "Forty-five, forty-six, forty-seven . . ."

Mom shrieked, "Silken! You're going to hurt yourself! Put down those weights—*put them down!* You'll ruin your figure!"

At first, Daniele and I just grunted in frustration because we were so intensely focused. Later, we fell into peals of laughter, remembering the horrified look on our mother's face.

SINGLE SCULLER

My innocent belief in the power and authority of the National Team training schedule proved well-founded. It overrode all my self-doubts so that I did make the National Team in 1983, on my first attempt. Then, in the summer of 1984, when I was nineteen, I fulfilled my most cherished dream: to compete in the Olympics.

In the Canadian trials for single sculls, Daniele had been positioned to win. I was her closest competitor, and was desperate to beat her. In a phone call to our dad, Daniele said she wasn't sure she wanted to race because she didn't want to defeat me. Her words still echo in my head: "I love winning, but I hate beating people."

Apparently, she didn't hate it too much. She soundly outpaced everyone in those trials, with me coming in second. Rowing Canada, in its wisdom, paired us to compete in Los Angeles in the women's doubles. We were horrified. Both of us were individualists in every way. We figured we might kill each other.

Daniele may have been the better rower, with more overall

strength, but I probably had a bit more dynamic power. While she was by far the more experienced tactician, I was certainly the more competitive one. In the lead-up to the Games, we had many sisterly quarrels.

Daniele would say, "Stop it! We're supposed to be rowing light."

"I *am* rowing lightly!"

"No, you're not, so stop it. You're making me look like I'm not pulling."

"I am not. You're just not pulling on purpose!"

The Olympics were held in Los Angeles that year. Because I'd been rowing only since 1982, everything that had happened during my accelerated buildup seemed brand new. Now, with the Games in the epicentre of show business, I was having both the Olympic experience and the Hollywood experience at the same time. Our residence was drenched in the pastel colours chosen by our hosts—melon, aqua, mint. After deboarding the bus at Lake Casitas, where our races were to be held, we walked across a bridge of floating docks to a spectacularly beautiful athletes' area with painted racks for every boat, a food court for post-workout snacks and several dipping pools to cool off in. The welcome centre featured video games along with big bowls of M&M's and Snickers—I felt like I was a kid in a candy store. On my first day, I was so afraid the bowls would empty that I filled a bread bag with the candy. The whole setup was surreal, like our very own Disney World.

My dad and brother had driven from Canada on a father–son road trip to watch Daniele and me race—it was for Joerg that I had hoarded the M&M's and Snickers. Both were very excited, especially when we gave them a tour of the Olympic Village, something that wouldn't be possible now with today's heightened security. Even then, every athlete had to have an identification pass for the village and boating areas. As the other rowers and I prepared to head for the lake in the wee hours of each morning, one of my biggest stresses became remembering my pass. After the security volunteers came to know me, they would ask before I left the grounds, "Silken, did you remember your ID?"

Daniele and I would be racing only 1,000 metres at the Los Angeles Games. When women's rowing was introduced into the Olympics in 1976, the organizers believed women couldn't handle the 2,000 metres that the men rowed. Even if we could, they figured that our races would be boring to watch, and that the time we'd need to complete the course would create scheduling problems for the men's races. It wasn't until 1985 that our international courses were extended to 2,000 metres. This opened up the playing field in an unexpected way, as it meant that the Russian and East German women's 200-pound, steroid-driven bodies would have to struggle to cover the greater distance.

I was scared to death as Daniele and I awaited the crack of the starter's pistol. Thanks to my highly strung novice state, we were sharp out of the gate. Although we settled into a good, aggressive middle pace, we failed to sufficiently lift our intensity for those last forty strokes.

We did make the podium for Canada with a bronze. It was incredibly exciting, despite the mixed feelings that come with racing. Winning a medal isn't like winning a lottery. Since Daniele and I had expected to medal, the bronze met our expectations but didn't exceed them. We were happy with our solid performance, yet we both felt we could have won silver if we'd rowed a perfect race. On the other hand, to medal at age nineteen with my sister, and to stand beside her on the podium as our dad and brother cheered, was pretty wonderful.

Our bronze win provided a high note on which Daniele could retire, while giving me a fabulous introduction to my future.

★ ★ ★

That fall, I moved to British Columbia to attend the University of Victoria, the only school to which I'd applied. It felt like a dream in so many ways: I could row while I pursued my education. And it fulfilled a promise I'd made to myself seven years earlier on one of those car trips with my dad. I'd stood under Vancouver's Gastown steam clock and vowed to live on the West Coast. I was serious about my academic studies, but Sport Canada's paying of my tuition and my taste of Olympic success meant rowing dominated.

In my first year, I roomed with Carla Pace, who was also on the National Rowing Team. Each morning when the alarm went off at six, I rolled off my futon, already wearing the first layer of my rowing clothing, the outer layers laid out by the door. I suppose this made for some stinky pyjamas, but the extra fifteen cozy minutes of sleep was worth it. Lisa Robertson, another National Team member, picked us up in her decrepit car so that we would be on Elk Lake while it was still dark. The car's front seat was propped forward with a broom handle, which one of us sometimes bumped, causing it to slip, launching the seat backwards. I guess this was dangerous, but we always found it hysterically funny.

The university took great pride in its rowing team—many of its members were already on the National Team—and I instantly became a part of the school community. Yet despite hanging out with the other rowers, I never totally felt part of the group because of the greater volume and intensity of my training as a single sculler. When I went out with them for what was supposed to be a steady-state row, I'd pull as hard as I could for fifteen kilometres, then climb from my scull red-faced and exhausted. My teammates probably thought I was out of shape if a ninety-minute, moderate-intensity row could leave me so wiped.

Being a single sculler also meant less camaraderie than if I were rowing doubles, quads or eights. Many rowers train as singles with the goal of qualifying for a crew boat, but for me it was the ultimate because it gave me that all-important control over my own destiny. When I watched the single scullers at the Olympics and World Championships, I dreamed that one day I would be standing on the podium as a single sculler representing Canada. To secure this position, I knew I had to be decidedly faster than any other rower in Canada, in every workout, in every race. It was as simple as that. The possibility of being placed in a boat with rowers with whom I couldn't mesh seemed a nightmare.

Single sculling also satisfied the part of my personality that wanted to remain a little aloof. I was always careful about whom I let into my heart. I didn't compete for UVic much, but I did row in a crew boat that won a big regatta in San Diego. That was like the Olympics for the rest of the team, so it was fun to share their excitement. I also enjoyed running, stretching and weightlifting with the other athletes, and sometimes congregating with them in the afternoon in the top foyer of the McKinnon Building.

My one major disappointment in that first year of university was my academic performance. In grade ten at Lorne Park Secondary School, a fabulous science teacher named Michael Bevan had turned me onto biology so much that my marks in that subject went through the roof. I became so excited about the beauty of living organisms, and how the different parts of a cell worked in wonderful harmony, that I decided I wanted to be a marine biologist. This required me to sign up for chemistry and physics and a bunch of labs and—*oh my God*—calculus, although I was so terrible at math.

As the dream of becoming a marine biologist fast-faded, the same stubborn aloofness that made me a single sculler prevented me from seeking academic guidance. Instead of formally dropping courses in which I was doing badly, I would just not attend, resulting in a mark of zero. By the end of my first semester, the pressure to keep up with my classes while rowing at the elite level brought my life to a crisis. One night after a chemistry exam, I lay sobbing on the campus lawn, feeling worthless and stupid. My reaction was even bigger than it might have been because my chemistry failure brought back so much of the pain I'd felt in childhood—when I'd struggled to learn to read, always confused, always failing, always wrong, always bad. Adding to my stress was the fact that things seemed rocky at home. Joerg was going through a phase of teenage rebellion and I felt guilty that I wasn't there for him. I was convinced that I was a loser in everything. I was exhausted from studying early in the morning and late at night, and from training twice a day—never mind from cycling as my main mode of transportation. Now, 4,000 kilometres from home and my network of friends, I didn't know how to ask for help or to whom I could reach out. I felt utterly alone and defeated.

After a few weeks of struggling against despair, I made a decision based on survival. I switched my major to English, which I loved, and in which I was an A student. I also dropped my courses down to three a semester. Although these changes felt like a defeat, they generated a new wave of enthusiasm for my sport as well as for my studies. I began to excel academically, and I never looked back.

It took courage to give up my dream of becoming a marine biologist, but the positive result of this decision confirmed my belief that I should always trust my gut instincts.

In the summer of 1985, I competed for Canada in single sculls, rowing 2,000 metres at the World Championships in Belgium. My technique was still pretty basic, but suddenly I was up against the best in the world. In the days before the final, my back spasmed, undermining my confidence. But even as a novice, I finished fourth—a result that both disappointed and thrilled me because it showed promise.

I was also put in a quad crew boat with Kay Worthington, Marilyn Campbell and Barbara Armbrust. They were terrific teammates, but the odds were against us: Marilyn and Barb were Olympic silver medallists in crew rowing but new to sculling; my persistent back injury was increasingly debilitating; and our coach liked to get into the heads of his athletes to break them down in order to build them up. His aggressive tactics didn't work with our group of powerhouse women, and we all suffered blows to our confidence. Barb finally called him out in a heated exchange.

But ultimately, because of my back spasms, we had to scratch. My dad, who had flown to Belgium to watch me row, arrived the day we withdrew from competition. I remember collapsing in his arms, sobbing in disappointment. I seriously considered quitting rowing that year.

In my second year at UVic, I not only did much better academically but also made a lifelong friend. After I kept falling asleep in one of my English classes, Kim Van Bruggen offered me her notes. We became friendly, and I invited her to a few parties and introduced her to rowing, where she met her husband.

Today, Kim's family and mine spend almost every major holiday together. She knows more about me than any other human being, and when Kim's mother died, I spoke at her funeral. We share interests like sports, yoga and books, but it's our spiritual journey that connects us most deeply. Our friendship touches my soul.

*   *   *

My continuing back problems prevented me from competing in the World Championships in 1986, and the following fall I transferred to Western University, in London. Joerg was rebelling in his teen years and I thought that if I were closer to home I could help. But then he dropped out of high school, took off across the United States on a motorcycle and moved to Florida, where our mother was by then living. I lost track of him for years. This was partly because I was self-absorbed, coping with such severe back trouble that people in the sport were predicting that my rowing career was over. To release my spasms I'd go to physio, which would shift the position of my pelvis, which would then exacerbate my sciatica, creating a vicious circle. Nobody had any answers, and nothing seemed to be helping. Then, partway through the first of what would be two years at Western, I contracted pneumonia. Here I was, in a city I didn't love, having changed universities in midstream, flat on my back in pain.

Eventually, I found a couple of specialists who taught me to manage my back. I also took up swimming, which I hated and was terrible at, but which was the only activity I could manage without pain.

As I later learned, my back had become hypermobile, so that my rotating pelvis was pressuring a nerve that was causing sciatica in my leg.

At the 1987 Pan-American Games in Indianapolis, I won gold in single sculls, putting me in striking distance for a singles medal at the 1988 Olympics in Seoul. Once again, I allowed others to override my own best instincts, leading to acute disappointment. In the 1985 World Championships, I had beaten Kay Worthington in single sculls by several seconds, coming fourth to her fifth. In Seoul, the coaches convinced me to row with Kay in the doubles instead of rowing singles. Disaster. We were like two bull moose in the forest. Both of us were individualistic in our rowing styles, both of us uncompromising. Plus I was still suffering back troubles. The repetitiveness of rowing meant that stroke after stroke I was pushing myself through the same agony—it was like having a blister and rubbing it a thousand times. That physical pain was infecting my personality, exaggerating my orneriness.

Kay and I came in a disappointing seventh.

From then on, it was singles for me forever and all the way. This suited not only my independent spirit but also my rowing technique, since I had a signature stroke that was different from that of other Canadian rowers.

Usually, as a rower's blades exit the water at the finish of a stroke, his or her body will be about 10 degrees past 90. Mine was pushed well back at more like 45 degrees, allowing me to use the weight and force of my powerful upper body for a little extra speed. There isn't anything right or wrong about this huge layback, and it came organically from my body. Because the ratio of my upper-body strength to my lower-body strength was high for a woman, I naturally gravitated farther into the bow, and when I tried to shorten the release, it hurt my back.

In the spring of 1990, my rowing career took off in an unexpected way that thrilled me. That was when I persuaded Mike Spracklen to be my coach, on the promise that the men's eight would be the priority. I gained not only Mike's expertise but also the camaraderie of the wonderful Canadian men's team, including that of my future husband.

Many people have tried to understand Mike's greatness as a coach. His training program was certainly challenging and relentless in its volume and intensity. He also took enormous care in making small adaptations based on what he witnessed every day from the coach boat, adding a long warm-down, shortening or cutting out a practice, or making a piece more competitive. As well as having tremendous skill in the technical aspects of rowing, Mike understands kinesthetics, which enables him to coach an athlete from the perspective of how it feels for that athlete to make a technical change. Many coaches can't grasp this. They can see where a person's technique differs from the ideal, but they have difficulty understanding how this might assist the athlete and why the athlete's body chooses to move in that specific way. Moreover, Mike can relate this in a way that connects the athlete to his or her body, helping to adapt a movement to make it more effective.

For years, coaches had been telling me, "Raise your hands at the finish of a stroke," "Feather your blade earlier," "Open your body angle sooner," and so on. It never worked because I couldn't *think* my way into a different style of rowing. Mike taught me how to *feel* my way into a new technique, how to move and act differently. Working with him was like discovering the sport for the first time. I learned about bell notes, the beautiful sound an oar makes when it exits the water absolutely perpendicular, without splash or a lip on the puddle. I learned about the moment of peace just before the oar enters the water, when the body is set and still, followed by a slight and subtle rising of the wrists. I learned how to breathe so that oxygen travelled into each section of my mighty lungs, and how to hold my body with poise through the searing pain of a sprint and the dulling heavy pain of exhaustion. From Mike I learned that each sensation has a name and a strategy for mastering it. Workout by workout I made friends with the bloody taste of fatigue in my mouth, with the intense cramping in my back and legs during a sprint.

Each day, the rawness of effort in a workout session was balanced by the grace and finesse of a technical session, during which Mike would spend forty minutes breaking down various components of a stroke for relearning. He helped me uncover a beautiful technique as if it were a treasure to be dug out shovelful by shovelful. I learned to feel the cues in my body and make the changes with which I'd struggled for years. These changes happened as if by magic—the kind of magic that's grounded in a staggering amount of miles on the water.

With Mike I was discovering a new language, a language of movement, of mental acuity. It was also a language of love, for Mike loved rowing with all his heart, and it showed in the way he approached the sport with passion, competitiveness and, yes, gentleness. He gave himself completely to it and to his athletes, so that I now fell in love with the sport in a different way. Rowing for me became animated, and my relationship to it more visceral yet also more nuanced. I growled with frustration when I repeatedly could not lift my blades off the water, and grinned with delight upon mastering something new. Each week, each day, took everything I had but gave me even more in return.

I wasn't the only one to benefit from Mike's attentive, highly personalized coaching. In the six months leading up to the 1990 World Championships on Lake Barrington in Tasmania, he transformed all our individual techniques to create a fit, well-trained team that rowed uniformly and powerfully.

Those championships in Tasmania, an island off the south coast of Australia, marked a watershed in my rowing career. The good stuff—the sweet stuff—began two weeks earlier, on the Yarra River in Melbourne, Australia. That's when my boat really started to sing. Thanks to Mike's instruction, I had found that fleeting place of rest in my stroke that for the first time made fast rowing feel effortless. As I pushed my oar handles down to lift the blades out of the water at the finish of a stroke, then began to swing my body forward for yet another stroke, I experienced a nanosecond of respite in that quarter of a breath before I dropped my blades back into the water—a quarter of a breath where I was fully relaxed. In this spot I was completely attuned to the speed and movement of the boat, so that all I needed was to drop the blade. That rhythm was everything, with that split second of recovery allowing for an explosive, dynamic stroke once the blade entered the water.

In those glorious weeks of training in Melbourne, I felt completely connected to my boat and oars. I felt confident not only that my body would find the most effective position but also that the boat would respond to my body's efforts. I've heard jockeys and equestrians talk about how their horses can read their bodies, responding to the slightest changes in pressure; in Australia, I felt I had built a relationship with my boat, so that it was an extension of my body. This was when I began talking to my boat, running my hands down its side as if petting a dog or horse, telling it how grateful I was for all the miles we'd shared. Maybe the sheer volume of training was finally getting to me.

Tasmania, where we practised from October 31 to November 4, two weeks before the 1990 World Championships, was a continuation of all the heady stuff I'd experienced in Melbourne. First, the island itself is a fantastical place of rainforests and waterfalls. Everything was gigantic, from the leaves on the trees to the brown recluse spiders and snakes that could kill you in a minute. After an hour's drive from

Launceston, our Canadian team's bus arrived at the top of a deep valley. We descended on a switchback road, the driver pushing the air brakes to slow down the bus. The road wound its way for about forty minutes, providing stunning views of the valley, not always appreciated by those of us who were green with motion sickness. Finally, we glimpsed a lake in the distance. As it came into full view, we could see that we would be rowing in Nirvana. By planting Lake Barrington in the middle of nowhere, God had created the perfect place for rowers to play, a body of water so gorgeous and flat it took our breath away.

This magnificence ended at the shore line. Our site lacked a permanent bathroom, a boathouse and a leisure area to hang out and get snacks. Each country had erected tents to protect its athletes and coaches from the harsh Australian sun, and somehow we wrestled army cots inside the Canadian tent for afternoon naps between practices. Each evening, we made the long drive up the switchback road back to Launceston.

Going into those World Championships, I was ranked seventh in single sculls, which was the best I could achieve in 1989, when I was still suffering from acute back pain. At Lake Barrington, I had a fabulous first heat, sending me directly into the semifinals. Then, in the draw before that race, I was unlucky enough to find myself competing with the gold, silver and bronze medallists from the previous World Championships: Elisabeta Lipa of Romania, Birgit Peter of East Germany and Tittie Jordache of West Germany. I had never beaten any of these athletes before, and now all three were queued at the starting line, with me having to finish in the top three to advance to the final.

Mike had instructed me to row out fast, then to move into my killer rhythm. If I was behind a competitor, I was to pull up beside that boat and imagine an elastic band connecting it with mine. I was then to row harder, feeling that band stretch as I opened the space between us until the elastic snapped and I'd left the competitor behind. Then I was to pull up to the next boat and do the same. This analogy may not seem so striking now, but it worked for me. Though I set a furious pace from the beginning, I never felt like I was rushing, thanks to that tiny rest with each stroke that Mike had taught me, which gave me a feeling of being in complete control. Mike had described this nano-rest as "one stop in," meaning that I was rowing the tiniest amount below full effort, so that I knew—but my competitors didn't—I had one more stop to go in the final sprint.

I was first across the finish line, having beaten all the medallists from 1989. I dropped my oars into my lap, flung up my arms with my palms touching as if in prayer and lifted my face to the heavens, my mouth open in surprise. Delight, terror, astonishment—so many emotions hit me at the same time. In that precise moment, I fully realized I could become the best in the world.

A photographer captured that image, and *The Globe and Mail* ran it on the front page the next day. Now I keep it framed in my office because it reminds me of how a single moment in time can open the door to a lifetime of possibility. Even though the race was only a semifinal, everything that proved extraordinary in my next six years stemmed from that day.

I still had the final to go. Two days later, I once again lined up with Elisabeta Lipa, the previous year's gold medallist, and

Birgit Peter, the silver medallist, on Lake Barrington. By the second half of the 2,000-metre race, I had rowed past both Elisabeta and Birgit to take a commanding lead. Going into the last 500 metres, Birgit began closing the gap. As her boat came closer, my confidence faltered. *Here was the famed East German powerhouse in full throttle! How could I hold her off?* Where the mind goes, the body goes. As the dialogue of doubt took over, my concentration faltered and my stroke lost its effortless fluidity. In the final 250 metres, Birgit breezed past me in a convincing sprint, beating me in the last twenty strokes.

I was thrilled to win silver—my first World Championship medal in single sculls—though I was aware with the brutal honesty required of an athlete that I had let myself down in those moments when I lost my confidence.

The trick in these circumstances is to be clear about what happened but not to make it mean more than it should so you end up engaging in non-stop self-criticism that harms more than it helps. Unfortunately, I was never very good at the latter. After losing in the final few strokes, I told myself I wasn't a strong finisher—a negative loop taking me down in a spiral that triggered all the vulnerability I'd felt as a child. No longer was this race about my performance; it became about all my horrendous shortcomings as a person.

Coaching isn't just about evaluating an athlete's performance. It's also about being alert to your athlete's psychological makeup, and to how he or she is likely to self-judge. Mike knew I was my own worst enemy, so he would always praise me at the dock with a hearty "Well done!" no matter how disappointed he knew I felt. Only after a few hours would we sit down to discuss the race, and then he would encourage me to talk about my experience—how I wasn't tough enough, how the pressure got to me. After that, he'd offer his own observations, including detailed advice about how we could work on the last 500 metres so I could become World Champion.

So much in racing doesn't meet the eye. Winning has as much to do with what happens in the first two minutes of a race as it does in the final twenty seconds. An athlete may have shot out of the gate a little harder than ideal in order to have a tactical advantage on a competitor because it seemed to be the only chance of winning, only to lose steam in the sprint. An intelligent coach must analyze strategy, psychology and performance. That Mike was good at analyzing all three was proven by the results the Canadians achieved at Lake Barrington: the men's eight with John Wallace also won silver, while the men's pair won bronze.

* * *

The 1991 World Championship at Vienna proved my time of triumph.

For six weeks of training, our entire team encamped at the Swiss village of Oberägeri, populated by only a few thousand people, on spectacular Lake Oberägeri. After my second-place finish in Tasmania, Mike and I spent a horrendous six weeks breaking down my stroke by keeping my body still at the front end while using the power of my legs to drive the blade. We relearned the stroke at the pace of 50 kilometres a day, many taken at slow speed as I grooved into this new approach. Our first workout of the day took place in the early hours of the morning, before a wonderful Swiss breakfast of Bircher muesli, fresh rye bread and chocolate milk. In those long hours of repetitive steady-state rowing, my mind would wander to the breakfast awaiting us, and often it was the image of that lovely muesli that got me through the workout. This mileage, added to my other training, meant my bottom spent six hours a day on a hard wooden seat, resulting in debilitating bone bruising. Seat pads helped for a few minutes, till they cut off circulation or rubbed my bruises in a different way. Mike would ask where I felt pressure from the seat, then carve a little from that spot, altering it slightly every couple of days in hopes of alleviating some of the pain for the next row. I don't know how much Mike's carving helped, but I will remember forever with gratitude him lovingly whittling away with his knife. I also remember, with somewhat less gratitude, the amusement of my teammates each night when I arrived in the dining room carrying my little pillow.

My loneliest time as a single sculler occurred at training camp that summer of 1991. Since the women were rowing with coach Al Morrow at completely different times, it was just me on the lake for the 20-kilometre workouts. Sometimes the two hours flew by as I focused on one technical bit or another; at other times, every lap seemed an eternity.

Single scullers have the extra pressure of relying only on ourselves as race day approaches, which means feeling the pressure build without being able to share it with a team. At the same time, I was at my peak as an athlete, so focused that all of life seemed to be happening at the end of an oar. The training load was brutal, lessened only by massages and physio, but my confidence and physical skill had never been stronger. Mike had a saying about how the stroke is one long, smooth, continuous movement, "always moving, never rushing." The catch where the blades enter the water, the drive where the legs, back and arms are pushing against the oar, and the recovery where the sculler moves forward in a defined series of relaxed movements, should all look and feel fluid. Between mastering the bell notes by consistently raising my oars clear of the water and finding some relaxation in my stroke, I felt for the first time in my career as if I was rowing with the speed of the boat rather than against it.

When a baseball player, seemingly effortlessly, strikes a ball at exactly the right spot on the bat so that the ball just sails away, it's called hitting "the sweet spot." With rowing, you may feel you've hit the sweet spot, so to speak, for a few days, or maybe even a few weeks, and then it eludes you for a few months. At this World Championship, I had hit the sweet spot, with no limit on how fast my boat could go.

One afternoon, in Sarnen, Switzerland, where we trained for two weeks that summer, our coaches, Mike and Al, decided to have Marnie McBean and Kathleen Heddle, the pair favoured to win gold at the upcoming 1991 World Championships, spar off with me. During our two-kilometre pieces, they were expected to be fifteen seconds faster than me, so rightly should have started behind me. We started together, and for the first 500 metres I wouldn't let them row through me. This was obviously grating on them, and I could hear Kathleen—usually a cool customer—and Marnie exchanging frustrated words. I was on fire, and upping the ante caused the friction between Marnie and me at that time. I really wanted to beat her. I was in my own world, willing to kill myself to stay ahead, no matter how tired I became or how much my body hurt.

When I trained with the men, occasionally that same competitiveness would overtake me. Once, while training with the men in Switzerland, I started to see red spots in front of my eyes, and without knowing what was happening, I lifted my head, became lightheaded and tumbled from my boat. I regained consciousness underwater. When I popped up my head, I saw Mike taking off his jacket to jump into the lake. I signalled that I was fine, despite having no recollection of falling out of the boat.

That workout stands apart from the thousands and thousands of them because I was on top of my game, driven by a superhuman force, pushing myself literally to the end of my physical limits.

It's another moment frozen in time.

* * *

On August 11, we moved from our Swiss training camp to Vienna for the 1991 World Championship, ten days before the competition was to begin. We were staying in a university dormitory much like an army barracks. The food was pretty awful, but it couldn't dampen my enthusiasm: Vienna was the most beautiful city I'd ever seen. I remember one evening in particular, having snacks and a hot drink in a rooftop café, the city laid out before us, and so much living happening high above the streets—in restaurants and gardens and on private patios and balconies, even on sloping roofs.

By this time, my focus on the competition ahead was laser-like. I visualized, literally thousands of times, winning gold, while also preparing myself mentally for every possible condition, upset or distraction. When I wasn't working out or strategizing the race, I was dreaming about it.

As always, a championship narrows down to one race. On the day of my final, I awoke to the sound of the howling wind. When I looked out the dormitory window, I saw that the branches of the trees were being blown sideways. I arrived at the course an hour later to see all the flags rippling fiercely and the water choppy. The person I had to beat to win gold was Elisabeta Lipa of Romania, one of the world's all-time great female rowers. She outweighed me by thirty pounds and was a good three inches taller—always a distinct advantage in rowing, but especially under these weather conditions.

Despite all my mental and physical preparation, I was very nervous in the warm-up. As I rowed steady-state along the Danube, I noticed a pregnant woman walking her toddler along the shore and wondered what it would be like to be her, to be anybody but me, with the pressure escalating. I reminded myself that I was exactly where I wanted to be, doing exactly what I had chosen to do for the purpose and privilege of fulfilling my ultimate lifetime dream. The routine of my warm-up soon settled my mind, though the adrenaline necessary for racing continued to surge through my body. I pictured my boat flying over the rough water.

At the starting gates, I felt calm and focused, and when the gun went off, I shot out, hungry for a win. It was another incredible race, the lead switching back and forth five times between Elisabeta and me, but with never more than a second between us as we pushed against the tough headwind. With thirty strokes to go, I took the lead one more time. Elisabeta broke, and I pulled away to win by three seconds. The joy of that victory was telegraphed by a smile that lit up my face for days, accompanied by an overwhelming feeling of satisfaction.

When I triumphantly mounted the podium in Vienna to accept my gold medal, I had no inkling of what lay just ahead—my injury at Essen, and the long, tough road to recovery. All I knew at that moment was that I was the fastest woman rower in the world.

Unlike those who'd predicted my career was over because of my back troubles, many of the people in my life had foreseen that moment well before I had. Even when I was still running track, Fred Loek, a local photojournalist who became my first rowing coach, believed I could be a World Champion in the single, and used to yell at me as I ran, "Try a real sport!" My dad had supported me with both money and enthusiasm throughout my athletic career, convinced that one day he would see gold in my hands. Mike had also believed in this victory well before it became a fact. My biggest obstacle had always been the self-doubt, so deep and so devastating, that kept whispering in my ear, *You're not good enough. You don't have what it takes. You don't deserve this.* Fortunately, I was possessed by an even stronger desire to win. The thought of being the best in the world at something had sparked my imagination when I was eleven, and then had kept appearing as a probability in some crazy way.

The little girl who was afraid to raise her hand in class, who struggled to find the confidence to ask for help when she needed it and who could be reduced to tears by a sharp word from a friend or even a complete stranger had clung to her ability to dream.

Part IV

SECOND CHANCES

LOVE

I n the summer of 2008, when I was forty-three, I met the love
of my life.

It started in an unlikely way. I was hired by a company
called canfitpro to speak at a conference in Toronto. The job
was a great fit for my schedule—my boyfriend at the time
and I could stop on our way home from a trip to Spain, so
I happily accepted. When I arrived at the conference, I met
David Patchell-Evans, the founder of canfitpro and GoodLife,
and gave him the attention I'd give any new client. He struck
me as poised and confident—the type of guy who set big goals
and was used to achieving them. But my interest in him was
strictly professional. I didn't think much of it, even though
I noticed that he was giving me *more* attention than I'd typically get from a client.

During a panel we both sat on, my view of him changed.
I talked about what I had learned about transitioning from
a single, intense focus on rowing to life as an inspirational
speaker, wife and mother. Patch talked at first about his interest in sports and charities—this seemed normal. He was a

successful guy discussing his successes. But then he surprised me by describing how his severely autistic daughter, Kilee, had taught him to become a better human being. He said that it had taken him years to establish a connection with her, but when she actually made eye contact and let him know she recognized him, it had been one of the most memorable moments of his life.

Patch spoke confidently without pretense, and with a ton of heart. He made an impression on me, but I still thought the connection was professional—and so was totally surprised when he gave me his phone number.

It had been six years since I'd split up with John, and I was in my second significant relationship since the split. The man I was dating was divorced like me, also with two kids. He was a coach, he loved music and he could talk about anything, including the books we shared. We enjoyed each other's company, and I had made a real heart connection with him early. However, it was becoming clear that while he wanted me, he wasn't ready to take on my kids, so our vision of the future was very different. Nevertheless, at the time of the conference, we were still a couple.

That fall, Patch did some detective work and tracked down my number. He phoned me a few times just to chat. He was playing it cool, as was I, so I didn't know his intentions. However, by the end of the year, Patch and I began to discuss having a first date. I was hesitant because my other relationship had ended and I didn't see how we could become a couple: he lived in London with shared custody of two children, while I lived in Victoria under the same circumstances. I continued to resist the idea of dating him, but Patch was persistent. In

April, he told me he would be skiing at Whistler later that month and suggested we meet in Vancouver. Travelling from Victoria to Vancouver for a first date seemed like a pretty big excursion, so I did a lot of hemming and hawing. In the end, I persuaded Kim and her daughter—my goddaughter, Kira—to accompany me so that if the date was a washout, the Vancouver trip wouldn't be a total loss.

Patch hadn't set a definite time and place to meet, so when I hadn't heard from him by four in the afternoon on the day we were to get together, I felt let down. He phoned at 4:35 and met me at my hotel, and we walked together to Cardero's, a restaurant on the waterfront. The late-in-the-day call put me off and left me with an impression that this was a guy who was used to having the world revolve around him. As I left the hotel, I said to Kim, "This could be a very short dinner. I may be joining you for the late movie."

I never did get to that movie. After about an hour of talking with Patch, I had a strong gut feeling that he was a special man.

And it turned out that we had a lot of similar experiences. I knew that Patch had been on Canada's National Rowing Team, but I hadn't realized how important the sport had been to him till he told me that his passion for rowing had inspired him to create GoodLife. Like me, he had had a devastating injury, in his case from a motorcycle accident that broke multiple bones and tore apart his shoulder. After eight months of intensive physiotherapy, he was inspired to switch to Western University's physical education program, where he earned an honour's degree.

The motorcycle crash wasn't the only tragic event in

Patch's life. At age eight, he had witnessed a car accident in which his dad was killed. Growing up poor with his mom and two brothers had spurred Patch to create a snowplowing business to put himself through university. Though his fleet of trucks, operated by his college buddies, kept breaking down, he made enough money to start what would become GoodLife. For that, he and his brothers hauled used exercise equipment in a dilapidated truck from Buffalo to London. Ironically, because of all this entrepreneurial activity, Patch was kicked out of his phys. ed. master's program for lack of focus. They told him that he needed to get his priorities straight. He did and started GoodLife Fitness.

When Patch and I met at the GoodLife conference, he had been in business mode, wearing an Armani suit and very much the corporate executive. I'd been hit on by powerful, self-regarding men before, many of them talking a good line about their achievements while having little in their lives that actually matched their boasts, and I think it was for this reason that I wasn't immediately attracted to Patch. But as I was to learn through our phone conversations that fall, Patch had not only built up GoodLife into a remarkably successful enterprise, he'd already begun to earn recognition for his leadership skills, being named *Canadian Business* magazine's Most Innovative CEO of 2005, followed the next year by induction into the prestigious International Entrepreneur of the Year Institute.

As for that Armani suit: it was a knock-off, as I discovered early in our conversation that night at Cardero's. Patch would spend money on experiences or his family without a thought, but an expensive status symbol like a power suit didn't even register on his list of priorities.

If Patch hadn't highlighted his relationship with Kilee at the conference where we'd met, I don't think I would have allowed our relationship to move to this next step. Now, as we both opened up about our families, I was once again impressed by his vulnerability and honesty. Like me, he'd had a partner who left him, creating a trail of hurt and confusion. As we discussed our parallel experiences, I recognized that here was someone with the capacity not only to feel but to grow.

Of special importance to me was Patch's interest in alternative healing, both physical and spiritual. He had taken a course in massage therapy that had opened his mind to the existence of forces and energies far greater than those we experience with our senses. After I had divorced John, one of the most exciting parts of my journey had been the renewal of my respect for my own inner wisdom. Patch also valued his instincts over his intellect in making important decisions. As we talked and talked, he delighted me with his curiosity about everything, with his love of life and with his willingness to take big risks.

I don't remember whether he and I kissed when we said goodnight. Probably I pecked him on the cheek. I do remember that I put my hand on his heart, really feeling this man.

When I got back to the hotel, Kim and Kira were already in bed.

Kim asked sleepily from under the covers, "How was your date?"

I replied, "He's the man I'm going to spend the rest of my life with."

That's when two heads popped up and the lights went on. "What?"

Kira, being only nineteen, wanted a rational explanation. "How do you know that?"

"I just do." My inner wisdom had told me that Patch was the whole package.

*   *   *

One very large obstacle stood in the way of our relationship: location. Patch still lived in London and I in Victoria. In the next few months, thanks to both our travelling, we managed to be in the same city about every three weeks or so.

In July 2009, Patch invited me to spend ten days with him and Kilee at his mother's cottage on Stoney Lake, the same lake where my family had once rented a cottage before my dad bought a place on Georgian Bay. The area had not been gentrified by the mansions and designer boathouses that now dotted Georgian Bay, and I felt an instant, nostalgic connection to its unspoiled beauty and laid-back atmosphere.

I had worried about meeting Kilee for the first time—that I wouldn't know how to interact with her or connect with her—but Patch was so fantastic with Kilee and she was in a great space that weekend. By then, I knew that I loved him, and we had begun to talk seriously about living together. We felt strongly that before we decided to do that, we'd better be very sure of our relationship. Too many other lives were involved to be trying this one on for size.

The idea that someday soon we would be partnered for the rest of our lives seemed both wonderful and crazy. Our bond was on every level: emotional, intellectual, spiritual. I wanted to spend every minute near him—even if we weren't speaking, we were connected. I felt like he wanted me for exactly who I was. For the first time, each of us had found a partner who was just as used to running the show—and for the first time, each of us found ourselves a little more (not a lot, though) willing to give to find middle ground. Our relationship was limitless in its possibilities, even though it offered plenty of challenges. I'd never felt so excited by and naturally connected to someone.

Later that summer, we decided to introduce our kids to each other during a day at Stoney Lake. William and Kate were twelve and nine; Patch's daughters, Kilee and Tygre, were fourteen and twelve. All of them understood that Patch and I were dating, but since both of us had introduced our kids to other potential partners, this was no big deal. They had plenty with which to amuse themselves, and the day was successful for everyone right up to the time we were getting ready to leave.

That was when Patch discovered he'd misplaced his car keys. And he'd lost his dog, a poorly trained St. Bernard who was as deaf as the proverbial post. Patch ran around, frantic about his deaf dog and swearing about his keys, while his ninety-year-old mother, Dorothy, turned over everything she could lift in an effort to locate them. But nobody could find either the keys or the dog, and we were forced to stay the night. My kids were in tears by then because they were overwhelmed and just wanted to return to Mississauga to be with their beloved opa.

The next morning, after a neighbour had found the St. Bernard wandering aimlessly two streets over, and after a set of keys had been delivered by a friend who'd driven four hours from London, Patch's mom asked me, in her no-nonsense way, "Are you sure you know what you're getting into?"

Today I understand that this chaos caused by lost items is rather typical of Patch, who hurtles ahead in a whirlwind, all passion and enthusiasm, but a little short on details.

★   ★   ★

Patch and I were growing closer and closer. Despite the physical distance, we were basically inseparable. But I hadn't brought myself to tell him about the darkness in my past. Even though I'd never felt so wholly loved and accepted, I worried that this small piece of me could change everything.

To tell this part of my story, I have to back up two years. Though Neil Tubb, my counsellor, and I had dealt with many issues, I still felt stuck. I was challenging myself to change in all the right ways, yet I was haunted by a sadness that never went away, especially during quiet times. After dealing with so much negative stuff, I thought I'd automatically feel good, but that wasn't happening. Too often I found myself lacking a sense of joy, feeling a bit lost and still unable to sleep properly. How could that be? When I was an athlete, I used to fall into bed, muscles heavy with fatigue, my face windburned from a day on the lake, then usually sleep like a corpse.

Far more troubling were the days when depression washed over me so deeply that I had trouble getting out of bed. Along with that depression came a dogged sense of guilt that I could feel this way when in all outward respects I had so much.

When I reached out to Neil for insight, he gave me advice for which I wasn't prepared: he repeatedly suggested that I try antidepressants. As he told me, "There's a chemical aspect to feeling good, and I don't think your liver is kicking out enough of the right stuff to raise your threshold."

I kept pushing away the thought. *Drugs—hadn't I already suffered enough when I took the Benadryl?* And then: *Wouldn't an antidepressant change my personality?* I remembered a friend who was hospitalized for what was then being called a nervous breakdown. Suddenly, everyone in our little community looked at this wildly funny, high-spirited girl as fundamentally different. A few took a protective role with her. Others became impatient with her bumpy road to recovery and just gave up on her. *Would taking an antidepressant stigmatize me, make my friends shy away? What about the people who looked to me for motivation?*

I consulted my GP for a second opinion. She suggested I take the antidepressant Cipralex for a three-week trial. After just three days, my spirits lifted significantly. I was no longer gripped by anxiety or pulled down by sadness. *Wow!* I thought. *Is this how other people feel all the time?*

Unfortunately, Cipralex produced an unpleasant side effect: night sweats. I switched medications several times trying to avoid this, but of them all, Cipralex still worked best for me emotionally. And I needed only a low dosage of it to feel a whole lot better. Whenever I tried to stop the medication altogether because I felt I'd resolved the underlying emotional issue, I had a terrible time with withdrawal. Antidepressants change your brain chemistry, which is the point of taking them. Quitting isn't like giving up Aspirin. I had headaches and dizziness and free-floating anxiety that left me feeling like a bundle of raw nerves. I'd hear my voice yelling at my kids and I'd think, *My*

God, here we go again. How did I get from zero to ten in no seconds? One day I nearly lost it with the vacuum-cleaner repairman, and in quiet moments, my sadness returned.

After I'd worked through a number of these cycles, my doctor recommended that I stay on the low dosage indefinitely. That made sense. I was in a good place, where I knew myself better and felt clearer about my goals. I was beginning to finally develop some real self-love and self-acceptance. Most importantly, my relationship with my children—my highest priority—had become extraordinarily good.

That was how *I* felt, but how was Patch going to feel about it? One of the things we both liked about each other and thought we shared was our belief in natural, alternative medicine.

While on a romantic weekend at a bed and breakfast, after a glass of wine and a fabulous meal, I confessed, "I take an antidepressant each day. It was a tough decision. I started about two years ago. I've tried to stop, but that never worked."

I was terrified that if Patch knew I battled depression, he might view me as mentally unstable and perhaps end our relationship. On the other hand, I knew I couldn't keep something this important from him. I also wanted him to know that I had tried two years of therapy before taking any medication; that my anxiety and depression were, in clinical terms, low level; and that both my counsellor and my GP felt my brain chemistry was at least partly at fault.

While I was making my little speech, Patch looked confused. Afterward, he kept asking me what I was like "normally," without any medication. *Does your whole personality change? Are you sure you need this medication? Have you tried better nutrition and positive affirmations?* He also expressed some of the same thoughts as my mom: *Why do you dwell on things that make you sad? If you want to witness real suffering, why not go to Africa?* In other words: *Think positively. Get over it.*

Patch was really struggling with the idea that this vivacious, energetic woman he loved could be depressed and anxious enough to need medication. I did a lot of educating that night and in the many months that followed, especially when Patch kept repeating his question about what my personality was like when I wasn't on medication. While this sometimes maddened me, I reminded myself that this was the same concern I had repeatedly put to Neil until my own experience had enlightened me.

It was tough to need to explain my choice to Patch and even to feel like I needed to apologize for it. I remember thinking that if I had sprained a finger I wouldn't need to explain putting on a splint. And that's how I'd come to think about our stigma with admitting to mental illness. If a friend had been hospitalized with a heart attack, or even with an illness brought on by abusing or ignoring his or her health, I would give that friend continued love and support as someone who's going through a rough patch. Yet when I was diagnosed with a mental disorder, that label felt poisonous. I worried I was in danger of becoming that diagnosis (and, frankly, I sadly still do worry, which is why I haven't told many of my close friends that I take a medication). But the reality is that most of us have bouts of sadness or periods when our emotions are out of control, making us vulnerable to traumatic events that rip us open and lay us bare, changing our brain chemistry and mental health. I told Patch that night how common it was:

one in five Canadians is hospitalized sometime during his or her lifetime for a mental illness. Hardly a rare disease. But the sting of having to admit it was part of our little world was tough for both of us.

*   *   *

Patch and I still had no specific future plans, though after five months of dating the only option we could see for being together was that my kids and I move to London, where GoodLife's head office was located. Patch's former wife, Tammy, who also lived in London, had married a man named Paul, and she she had two young children in addition to Kilee and Tygre, of whom she and Patch shared custody.

But there was a catch: before William, Kate and I could move, we would need John's consent. Our hope was that he'd agree to move to London as well. As far-fetched as this might now seem, I hoped it would be a possibility since we were both originally from Ontario and John was in a moment of transition. I thought a move east, closer to his family, might be something he would consider. However, John told us that he loved Victoria and wanted to stay on the West Coast so that he could be closer to his daughter, who lived with her mother, Jessica, in Calgary.

John and Jessica had a complex relationship, and while John was a loving father to his daughter, Jessica had sole custody.

I asked John if he would consider asking Jessica to move to London, where we could all be together. He suggested I should ask her.

And so I did.

By now, Jessica and I were on friendly terms. I respected her commitment to his daughter, and we had a bond because we both had children with John. I also felt that Jessica was genuinely supportive of Patch and me. She knew we had fallen in love and were having heated conversations with John about moving.

Patch arranged for Jessica to be interviewed for a job with GoodLife as an inducement for moving to London. That's when John seemed to stop even considering leaving Victoria. To be entirely fair, John had been more than flexible in negotiating our schedule with the kids, which had revolved around me and my work and travel schedule. Suggesting he move, no matter how much sense it made in my head, was a big ask. And so Patch and I came up with a few different proposals, trying to be as generous and creative as possible in hopes that he would change his mind. If he chose to stay in Victoria, we offered to fly him from Victoria to London every month, and give him summers with the kids in Victoria to make up for having less time with them during the school year. We would take the kids to London for two years, then move back to Victoria with them for two. None of these scenarios was ideal, but Patch and I were desperate to find a way to move forward.

My strong belief is that family disputes like ours don't belong in court, but John wouldn't budge and I had run out of options. I initiated legal proceedings, seeking my right to mobility. For the next eighteen months, John and I became caught up in a legal struggle—court dates, judges, lawyers—in which all the bitterness we'd managed to sidestep during our divorce was belatedly played out.

It was an awful time of stress and conflict for everyone.

John feared being forced to move from Victoria, or worse, having his kids move without him. I was taking a stand for my own happiness and felt that moving gave all of us the added benefit of being close to both sets of relatives.

In the end, Jessica decided she didn't want to move to London: she turned down GoodLife's offer of employment there, but said yes to an opportunity to work for GoodLife in Calgary, where she wanted to remain.

During this very trying period, Patch and I were meeting in various places and creating as much of a life for ourselves and our kids as we could. Kate and William knew that their dad and I were fighting over my desire to take them to London, and no doubt could feel the tension escalating. I tried to explain to them that this was an adult problem, but of course they understood that any resolution affected their lives as well. I assumed they would prefer to stay in Victoria rather than be uprooted, though they never said anything more to me than "Dad doesn't want to move." I was also confident that once they settled in London they would be just as happy there as in Victoria.

In May, our case was heard in the BC Supreme Court. I told the judge that I would not move—I *could not* move—without my kids. John said he would not move even if the kids moved. The judge decided in favour of John, which in many ways he had to do to preserve family solidarity.

Both Patch and I were devastated. I was also furious at John for what I saw as his inflexibility and meanness. I appealed to the BC Court of Appeal for the right to a new trial with the aim of reversing the lower court's decision, and it was granted. I thought John might now agree to move, to preserve a steady relationship with our kids, rather than going through the same pressure and turmoil all over again. He wouldn't budge, and in the end, I gave in before we went back to court. I threw up my hands. "Enough! I'm stopping."

The prolonged battle had become toxic for our children, and now John was so infuriated, it could only become worse. I felt I must stay in Victoria for our kids' sake. Patch felt the same about staying in London for his kids' sake. So after eighteen months of wrangling, we were all in a holding pattern, with no solution in sight.

That was when something utterly unexpected occurred.

The London Free Press printed a gossipy story that got picked up by the wires. It was written from legal documents, about our marital soap opera. Patch's ex-wife, Tammy, read the article, and suggested to Patch that she might be willing to move.

We were flabbergasted. Tammy had grown up in London, where she ran a dance studio. Her family still lived there, and all four of her children had been born and raised there. She had a deep connection to the city, yet she and her husband were willing to consider making this big change that would help Patch and me tremendously. She and Paul flew with their kids to Victoria to check it out, then decided they would be happy living here.

Now it was Patch who was faced with a big paradigm shift. The head office of GoodLife with its staff of 250, governing 10,000 employees across Canada, was in London. For him to move to Victoria had huge professional implications, including a new and exhausting travel schedule. Patch made the tough decision to pay that big price so we could all be together.

* * *

In the middle of the court battle, it had been tough to see how anything good could come out of something so difficult. But my connection with Patch was so strong that I knew in the deepest way I'd made the right choice. He was a partner who would stand beside me no matter what, and there was an odd part of me that felt blessed to have had our relationship tested in such an intense way so early—and to emerge so strong. As hard as it was, I knew that this new happiness I had found was worth it, and that I'd never look back.

BUILDING A NEW FAMILY

Once the smoke of our court battles had cleared, Patch and I switched our focus to building the right kind of life for our new blended family. I'd spent seventeen years in the house in Victoria that I'd initially purchased with John, but it wasn't right for this next chapter in our lives—practically, it just wasn't big enough, and emotionally, I was craving a fresh start. So Patch and I decided to purchase a home together and put my house on the market. While Patch transitioned to running his business remotely, I focused on the physical footprint of our lives.

My old house sold quickly, and we soon found an oceanfront place that was dated but had great bones. So before I knew it, I found myself saying goodbye to a place that had seen me through nearly two decades of change and growth. I wandered through the garden I had tended for so many seasons, saying goodbye to its well-loved inhabitants—the magnolia tree by the kitchen window that each April reminded me it was spring; the giant poppies the burst forth each May in an explosion of scarlet, so fleeting that if I made a business trip at the wrong time, I would miss them. That spring, I saw one of the pods break open and a poppy emerge, waving its petals as if to say goodbye. I knew that I was moving to a fresh and beautiful garden with different flowers and trees, but I wanted to remember the old friends who'd inspired and delighted me.

Because Patch was in London, and William and Kate were with John, I actually spent my first night alone in the new house. That evening I sipped a glass of wine on the porch, in awe of the view of the ocean. It was the middle of June and stunningly beautiful. Despite being alone, I knew that I was blessed to be here and I felt connected to the space in an incredible way. It was already home.

Smokey, my cat, didn't click quite so instantly with the place. He howled all that first night, his screeching marring the blissful ocean quiet I'd imagined, then ran away for a full three months a few days later. If I were in a different head space, this might have felt like a bad omen to me, but at the time his cries just felt like an acknowledgment of how totally different things would be from here on out, even if we'd only moved a few kilometres.

I woke up the next morning to a hot summer day. William and Kate arrived and the three of us discovered our new home. We ran screaming through the halls in the silliest game of tag you could imagine and then slept in the master bedroom's walk-in closet. It was a tight fit with all three of us and our blow-up mattresses, but we cozied up and watched DVDs. Even though leaving the only home they'd known was a big deal for William and Kate, that night was an adventure—just the three of us, explorers camped out in our new little world.

We started renovations within a week. The changes we needed ranged from modifications to make the layout work for Kilee to the addition of more bedrooms to ensure that all four kids could be comfortably at home. Patch had agreed to take full custody of Kilee, so she would be with us full time, William and Kate half the time and Tygre one third of the time. I should have seen it coming, but the tensions that erupted over who would get which bedroom caught me by surprise. The kids seemed focused on whether things were "fair." Whose room was biggest? Why did Kilee get her own bathroom? Did it really make sense that William got the biggest room just because he was oldest? It quickly became clear to me that these negotiations were about something much larger—each of our children wanted to know that she or he was just as important as the others, belonged as much as the others, was given as much space to grow as the others. So I listened and found my model for parenting in a blended family situation where four kids have very different needs: I can't make it so that everything is exactly *fair* (oftentimes Kilee's needs mean that she gets more attention and more resources), but I can always ensure that our kids have been *heard* and acknowledged. Their feelings are worth my time, and I try to go out of my way to make sure that they know it.

The renovations lasted from July through October, and the months of stressing over room assignments and paint colours were entirely worth it. Our house was now a beautiful home, and once Patch, Kilee and Tygre arrived we turned our attention from building the house to building a family. Both Patch and I were intent on creating shared experiences and memories for us as a group, so when we realized that our first weekend all together would coincide with what was supposed to be a record salmon run in BC's interior, we flew together to go see it. The trip was an epic disaster—it was just too much change for Kilee, and she was inconsolable. We haven't given up on creating special memories—we love to surf, ski, travel and just hang out at the house watching movies together—but that trip was a needed reminder that having Kilee at the centre of our lives means that sometimes our plans will get changed or an outing will become a disaster.

Bringing together two families with different styles has meant a lot of negotiating. Kate, William and I tend to be very loud and boisterous—we'll yell if we're happy or if we're angry or even if we're just at different ends of the house. For Patch, Kilee and Tygre, yelling signalled conflict and was something to avoid. So we've tried to find middle ground and new ways of communicating. We've also worked hard on establishing boundaries, especially in regard to Kilee's behaviour. Patch was always used to everyone moving around Kilee to accommodate her outbursts. But I've insisted that the rest of the family has the right to remain where they are, and that Kilee can be the one (gently) removed from a troublesome situation. It's a little thing, but it's one way I've tried to ensure that Tygre, William and Kate understand that they are incredibly important to us, even when Kilee might need our full attention. This care with the small details has been helpful in building my own relationship with Tygre. At first, I think she was uncomfortable expressing how she was feeling about all of the change. She wasn't sure where she stood among all the chaos. But over time, she's seen that I'll try to stick up for her when her dad is being overprotective or unreasonable with his expectations, and that I have her best interests at heart when I encourage communication between her and her dad on thorny topics like arranging her schedule with us.

And it's those details we've found hardest—the nitty-gritty of who will be where when and who is picking up whom (or not) at soccer or rowing. Our lives are complicated. Kilee requires twenty-four-hour supervision, and so coordinating Kilee's nannies, doctors, therapists and nighttime caregivers is an ongoing, busy job. Being a sister to Kilee has not been an easy job. Tygre has her energy into excelling at school and dancing each night of the week. Dance has been a place for Tygre to go where she is separate from Kilee and can be the centre of attention in her own way. William is involved in rowing and rugby. Kate runs track and does synchronized swimming. It's nearly a full-time job to keep track of their schedules. And yet, it's managed by perhaps two of the best-meaning but least routine-oriented adults you might ever meet. Patch can sometimes get caught up by his passion for work and his tendency to overcommit. With me, it's my obliviousness to time, my inability to sort and file and to say no when I'm already overburdened. So yes, overcommitment, too. I left Kilee stranded at school once and learned from that day on that I must write things down because my brain just can't hold all the little details.

*   *   *

It was Kate who taught us all some of our best coping strategies, in the most unexpected way. From the day Kate was born, I knew that she was an unusually active child, and it soon became clear that she was also an unusually vocal child. When she spoke too loudly or too fast, or interrupted others repeatedly, or when her teachers complained she was disturbing the class with her inability to sit still, I had always felt that my parenting skills must be lacking. The penny didn't drop for me until Kate was seven. We were driving in the car, and she asked me, "Mommy, have you ever noticed how the brain is always talking, talking, talking? Even when I'm sleeping, my brain is talking."

I booked a pediatric appointment. Three months later, I found myself sitting across from a doctor who delivered a disturbing diagnosis: Kate had attention deficit disorder (ADD), characterized by hyperactivity, distractibility and impulsiveness. Although I'd suspected this, I was numb when I actually heard the words. The pediatrician was confident of her diagnosis and suggested putting Kate on medication. I was horrified: *What kind of mother puts her nine-year-old on medication?*

Patch and I had arrived at the doctor's office in separate cars. After the appointment, I was so distraught at the diagnosis that I couldn't remember where I had parked. Patch had to run the neighbourhood blocks looking for my car. As I walked around in circles, I began second-guessing both myself and the doctor: *Maybe if I had been home more when Kate was little, she wouldn't have ADD now? Maybe if I give her more consistent boundaries she won't need medication? Or maybe if I send her to a different school?*

Complicating the situation for me was the fact that I had publicly expressed strong opinions about what I felt was the overprescribing of drugs to hyperactive kids suspected of ADD. I'd written articles putting forward my simple, heartfelt solution to what I saw as behavioural issues: more fresh air and exercise. But Kate already walked a mile to school every day, participated in sports four nights a week, rode her bike in the evenings and hiked on weekends.

I have always loved Kate for exactly who she is. I couldn't ask her to be less animated or energetic or opinionated. She was born strong and vibrant. Yet as she moved through the school system, it became apparent that for her to excel, we were going to have to help her become aware of some behaviours and attitudes that didn't serve her well. She had to learn that randomly doing a cartwheel on the gym floor might be distracting for the teacher and the other students. She had to learn that speaking loudly made it hard for others to concentrate.

Medication was not what I wanted for Kate, but I also knew that she deserved some mental peace. She deserved to be seen for her incredible gifts rather than for the problems that her teachers and coaches constantly claimed she was causing. She deserved to be given help to succeed. My own experience with medication helped me to understand, in my heart of hearts, that the doctor might be right. Kate needed structure and exercise, but she also needed medication.

Kate's teachers noticed a difference right away. Both her grades and her behaviour improved, and she seemed to be enjoying her classes more. She no longer seemed so overwhelmed by the intensity of her emotions. The change wasn't hugely dramatic, like a neon sign suddenly flashing, but we could tell the difference if we accidentally missed the daily dose. At first, Kate had fought against taking medication—until she felt that it was helping her. Then she became the one vigilant about taking it, saying, "I have a test today, Mom. I need my pill."

Just as I had trouble learning to read, so did Kate. The difference is that she was given a useful diagnosis alongside her diagnosis of ADD: dyslexia. Although she had some fabulous teachers in her public elementary school, just as I did, eventually I came to the conclusion that the educational structure wasn't flexible enough for her. She is now attending an outstanding private middle school, which I'm grateful we can afford, and it offers her greater opportunities for movement and creativity. She has discovered that sitting on a physio ball allows her to burn extra energy, making it easier for her to pay attention—I remember my agony trying to sit still as a kid and can only wonder how this kind of small change would have helped me academically. I've also shifted my mindset in the way I view and celebrate academic success. In our household, A grades in art, in choir, in physical education, in drama are equal to those in math or in English.

Despite being dyslexic, Kate believes that she can be and do anything. She may always misread the words "dread" and "bread," but already she writes plays, makes films on her iMac and enjoys many of the same books as her friends do, with the aid of audiobooks. Her future is wide open, and she can, and will, do anything to which she sets her mind.

Instead of allowing Kate to be defined by a label, I prefer to educate others about neurological disorders. I've also learned to take the gift in whatever package it is wrapped. Kate may need two thousand words to tell me about her day, but when I turn off my desire for her to condense and edit, and I really listen, I discover a great window into her spectacular imagination, her social relationships and the way her mind works. One night I was helping Kate visualize her "happy place." To get her started, I told her mine: I imagined myself sitting at the foot of a lovely old oak tree that stands at the top of a hill, the wind rustling its leaves, making me feel at peace. It took me about ten minutes just to get Kate still enough to find her happy place, but when she did, she told me about a waterfall with big, soft, white pillows behind it, where she could sit and watch a unicorn drinking water, and some goldfish with wings.

At the age of twelve, Kate decided that she no longer wanted to take her medication. So far that has worked well. Possibly she has developed better coping methods through a greater understanding of herself. Whatever she decides, I will stand by her.

Kate was initially very private about having ADD because, like me with my depression, she was afraid that her friends would view her differently. Slowly she came to understand that every brain is unique, and that this is what makes us all so interesting. My friend Jake Wetzel, who also has ADD, not only became an Olympic gold medallist in rowing but also began a PhD in finance at the University of British Columbia. Jake, who is pretty much a genius, made Kate feel special whenever he spent time with her, giving her the confidence to become an advocate for others. Now she allows me to talk about the issues we face as a family in order to help those struggling with the same problems.

Fortunately, Kate has the gift of self-awareness and an amazing ability to communicate. She has become fearless in telling her teachers, her coaches and me what she needs to function efficiently. She tells me that it stresses her out to be told to do more than one thing at a time—something I can relate to. She asks me to put a note beside the front door, reminding her to take her glasses, her bag for synchronized swimming, her homework. What we've found is that Kate's coping strategies work well for our family as a whole, so that Kate's knowledge of herself and her needs has helped us create a system that allows us all to navigate the chaos of so many big, busy lives coming together.

* * *

William has played an equally important role in bringing together our families. At sixteen, William is tall and lanky and laid-back in comparison with the rest of us. He is quick to smile and has a gentleness that people notice. He is the glue that has really brought all four of our kids together—even when he is mercilessly teasing his sisters. It would be hard to find a bigger-hearted boy his age. But his easygoing demeanour hides a real determination to achieve his goals. I find it's just so easy to be in his company—whether we're going for a boat ride or walking the dogs together.

It was through William that I reconnected to the world of sport as more than a spectator. I had loved my involvement in rowing, but I had spent so long living that lifestyle that it no longer captured my imagination. Given that William is the son of two Olympians, no one was surprised when he took up rowing in middle school—except for me. The rule in our house is that you must choose a sport every season, but which one is entirely up to you.

William was one of thirty-two middle-school boys and girls who had never rowed before. They had one paid coach but needed volunteers, so I agreed to help out even though

I thought I might well be courting a migraine. I plunged in, ready to make the best of it, only to discover I was having fun. In ten weeks I saw the kids go from not knowing how to hold an oar, or how to tell the difference between the front and back of the boat, to actually rowing in an eight crew for 500 metres without stopping. I saw their pride when they learned what they could achieve by pulling hard, and the amazement on the faces of these "non-athletes" when they uncovered their talent. William's competitive nature is a little below the surface, yet he pushes himself harder with an oar in his hand than in any other sport. And he is strong.

On the weekend of our first regatta, some of the boys were putting their boat into the water when they discovered it was broken. The team was given another boat, but that, too, had mechanical problems. Then, when we were preparing to launch a third boat, we were told we were too late: the race had already started. It was a huge disappointment for my young crew and frustrating for me as coach. I took this opportunity to talk about all the factors rowing participants can't control—the weather, the lanes, the other competitors in the same heat. I talked about the importance of staying positive and of using only respectful language with the officials and the organizers. My hope was that they would remember these words longer than the sting of missing a race. As luck would have it, they were able to compete later in the day, and they finished fourth, actually beating one of the high-school crews. The boys were thrilled to see how frustration could turn into an opportunity, and I was thrilled to have the privilege of translating my years of rowing into a life lesson that I could pass on.

Contrary to what I had imagined, I loved coaching these young kids precisely because I was giving them their first experience of a sport I adored, not trying to turn them into elite athletes. Give my own addiction to perfection, I sometimes had to be reminded of this. As William put it to me, "Mom, you're used to rowing at a high level. You're not as good coaching at my level because you expect too much." That reminded me to pay more attention to the individual athletes, as Mike Spracken always did, and to tone down my emphasis on technique.

John also volunteered to coach William's crew. It was healing for us to work in pursuit of the same goals, no matter how low-key, and probably even more healing for William. Should William continue to row, I hope he will continue to discover the thrill of setting and achieving goals and of forging deep friendships, while also building confidence to take risks and survive failure. I know this will result in greater discipline, focus and fulfillment in all other areas of his life.

Kate is also a talented athlete—an all-rounder who's good at dancing, who's passionate about synchronized swimming and who's a fast runner, fuelled by a competitive nature that has her pushing hard to win. Instead of having a single focus, she is endlessly interested in new things.

A confession here: just as I had to live with a mother who was constantly stealing the spotlight, so my kids have had to live with a mother who, even at school functions, is approached by people who want to take her picture or get an autograph. I believe Kate and William are confident enough to roll with this, though my renown has made me more hands-off when it comes to their activities than I otherwise might have been. Though I loved coaching William, I stayed back from it more than I wanted to because I knew he needed to establish this sport as his own, not as an extension of his mother's or his father's world. When I did attend regattas and attracted attention, William made a point of hanging out with his teammates. At one regatta, when I went to his dock because I knew the dock marshals, William chided me, "Why can't you stay on the shore like all the normal parents?"

So there it was, spelled out for me: my kids were seeing me as the world's pushiest and most embarrassing mother, just how I saw my own mom. The difference is that they lay down rules for me, even though I can sometimes wrangle for more space. After a season of self-banishment, my son accepted that in the rowing world, I wasn't a "normal" parent, since I usually knew most of those in charge—which has its advantages for him, as well as its disadvantages.

* * *

That lesson of giving space while still being true to myself is one I've tried to carry over into all aspects of our family life. When we first all came together, I tried to manage everything to make sure that it was perfect. I felt as if somehow the perfect throw pillows or the perfect piece of art in the perfect place would translate into a perfect family. Now I don't want a "perfect" family—I want *our* family, messy but honest and completely loving.

AUTISM

The first time Kilee attacked me, I did everything a person shouldn't do. We were sitting together on the couch reading stories, about a year into my relationship with Patch, when she started to obsess about a scab on her lip. I reached for her hand to draw it from the scab and she freaked out. She started biting her own hand, then grabbed a hunk of my hair. My adrenaline shot through the roof, as if I were being attacked by a mugger in a back alley. I went into survival mode, pushing her back hard, then grabbing her arms and digging in my nails so she'd release my hair. At the same time, I shrieked, "Stop it, Kilee! Stop it!"

She screamed even louder than me, causing Patch to rush into the room to see what was happening to his two out-of-control loved ones. By the time he'd separated us, we were both crying—Kilee out of remorse and me out of rage.

For the next two hours, every time Kilee saw me she'd burst into sobs. I'd do the same until my adrenaline kicked in again, causing me to alternate between fury and feeling overwhelmed. Somewhere in the midst of all this, I started packing my bags. I told Patch, my voice seething with accusation, "I'm getting the hell out of here until you can get your daughter under control!"

Thank goodness my next decision was a rational one: I phoned my counsellor.

Neil reminded me that my fury was a chemical reaction to a threatening situation, and that anything I said or did while under its influence would not be constructive. Of course, he was right. I could feel the adrenaline coursing through my body like a freight train, the way it used to when I was preparing for a big race. Neil's words about what was happening to me on a cellular level, so matter of fact, soothed and silenced the negative voice in my head judging Kilee, judging me, judging Patch, my lover and best friend.

Neil advised me to go for a workout or a long walk. I went out the door—okay, maybe I stamped out—and took a long hike, ending at Starbucks for a tall cappuccino, which I consider another reasonable answer to many of life's problems.

Once back home, I made a second good decision: not to talk about what had happened with Kilee. My thinking is too drastic when I'm throbbing with emotion, so it's better for me to cool my jets for twenty-four hours, until I'm calm enough to have a constructive conversation. By then, Patch, my problem-solving partner, has usually figured out some way of changing our world to make it better.

* * *

When Patch first told me about Kilee, then age twelve, I had felt something resonate for me on a spiritual level. Perhaps that was because my teenaged desire to cut myself allowed me to understand the pent-up emotions that led Kilee to bite her hand till it bled. When she banged her head on the ground, giving herself a goose egg, I was reminded of the day I'd banged my head on the wall outside the hotel room in which I'd locked my children to protect them.

When Patch took sole custody of Kilee about a year after we met, I didn't think I would find it a huge leap to care for her full time. I was wrong.

Kilee is a now a sixteen-year-old with a significant cognitive disability that reveals itself in an incapacity to remember how to do simple tasks or to retain the most basic information. When she becomes frustrated she also becomes aggressive, and because, at 170 pounds, she's bigger than me, with huge shoulders and a strength she doesn't moderate, she can be very frightening. Sometimes I'm scared by the degree of chaos I have taken on. Sometimes I'm ashamed at how frustrated I feel with Kilee and my desire to fling blame. When I'm forging ahead on a project and she obsessively asks for the ninetieth time for some object she's become fixated on, I must take a lot of steps back and remember how powerless she is to control her life, and how dependent she is on us to nurture and provide for her. She is more vulnerable than most two-year-olds, and the love that I give her must be as unwavering as my love for my own kids—relentless, fierce, unconditional. When I manage that, Kilee brings out the best in me. Then, I can be astounded at the patience I have in taking her for an hour-long walk, during which she tells me non-stop that she wants her boots off or is "very, very hungry," or that she wants her dinosaurs—the plastic toys with the chewed-off legs and heads that are her comfort objects.

It's always hard to get Kilee to change an activity. If she's on the couch playing with her dinosaurs, my asking her to go outside raises her stress level to the point of her biting her hand or stomping off. Once she's out there—walking, or boating, or swimming—she has a marvellous time, and I'm sure that physical exercise and fresh air have a calming effect on her, just as they do on the rest of us, even when we have to push ourselves out the door.

Patch says that when Kilee was first diagnosed as autistic at thirty months old, he and Tammy were told that if they did everything right, she could be cured. Believing this, Patch set up a playroom designed by a team of volunteer therapists, and he held his business meetings at home instead of going to the office.

Kilee was put on a special diet, then given physical therapy, cognitive therapy, play therapy, behavioural therapy. Mostly, she was home-schooled using the internationally acclaimed Son-Rise Program for those with developmental difficulties. Later, she worked with a skilled and unflappable specialist, Jonathan Alderson, using a multi-disciplinary approach. It all helped. After three years, she could sit at a table and eat with others. She could access enough words to ask for what she needed. She was able to sleep independently, with few fits of screaming. By the time Kilee was seven, all those involved in her care agreed she had made good progress, but she certainly wasn't cured. She wasn't even what the literature describes as "high functioning."

Because of the complexity of autism, the terms "high" and "low" are at best a loose way of designating where someone is on the autism spectrum. Kilee's IQ has tested at thirty, which is where she operates in some ways, while in other ways she is far smarter than such a limiting test can measure. Because she has a passion for food, she can name every item she has ever eaten. She can also be very persistent about exactly what she wants. On one occasion, she persuaded her special-needs ski instructor to buy her french fries and a Rice Krispie square, even though he knew this was forbidden. One of the special-needs girls with whom Kilee dances has the same obsession with food. The first time she was in our home, she kept insisting, "My mother doesn't feed me, my mother doesn't feed me," until I broke down and gave her a bowl of cereal.

Patch carries both pain and guilt because he couldn't cure Kilee or make her independent, despite his Herculean efforts, his boundless love and his extraordinary drive. Many parents with special-needs children carry that same guilt, which I understand because I felt it with Kate until I became better informed. Now, being with Kilee stirs up the usual self-scrutinizing questions: *Maybe I could redesign the household routine for her to make her more independent? Maybe I could secure more consistent caregivers? Maybe I could find her a more suitable school? Maybe I could have prevented this morning's food grab if I'd been in the kitchen instead of writing this book?*

Some people have called me a saint for my voluntary role in helping to raise Kilee. My response is "No, I'm not. I have bad thoughts." I shrug off the label as surely as I would the label of "demon." I have moments when I really don't like Kilee, days when her hours of asking for something makes me angry and I have to leave the room to find my patience again. At those times, I remember the words of a dear friend with a special-needs son: "We are good people, doing a good thing, but it's so easy not to feel good and to see everything from a negative viewpoint."

So, yes, Kilee took some getting used to, but now I can take her to a restaurant, or a movie, or a public swim, just the two of us. I can also see that she possesses a beautiful and gentle soul, and though language is difficult for her, she continues to find new words to make herself understood by those who know her.

Sometimes I need a break from her needs, her constant requests, and my worry about what she might do next. However, most of the time I'm able just to love her with the judgment peeled away. She is Kilee, with all her special needs and dependencies, with her sense of fun, her tenderness that expresses itself in the request "I need a cuddle." She makes me laugh and she makes me scream—silently now.

Kilee constantly surprises me. On Patch's iPad, she learned to play the game Angry Birds in ten seconds flat. When we gave her an iPod for her birthday, she learned how to use the touch screen more easily than her dad. Now she scrolls through her music, stopping on her favourite tunes. She also easily learns the new games William downloads for her.

My birth children's relationship with Kilee is absolutely wonderful. William is her protector, her advocate, her friend. He is tender and kind with her, and I see his emotional intelligence growing in leaps and bounds, thanks in part to the time he spends with her. Once when I became concerned for him because Kilee was trying to grab his hair, he told me that he wasn't frightened of his stepsister, and that he could remain calm when she threw a tantrum. When I suggested that I should learn from him, he replied, "But Mom, it's totally different for you. You have to protect us. That's your job."

To know that William was so clear that I would stand up for him, so clear about the stresses of parenting, so clear about his own feelings toward Kilee was heartwarming. He is constantly pointing out Kilee's new-found skills to the rest of us, and on the rare occasion when he's irritated by her, he'll say to me, "She's driving me crazy asking for her dinosaurs and her olives. I'm going upstairs."

Kate took a while to warm up to Kilee. Since she is less than half Kilee's weight, her wariness of Kilee's bursts of frustration, her tantrums and her hand biting was well-founded. Kate is sensitive to other people's energy, so she is often able to warn me that Kilee is about to have a meltdown before I notice the signs. Now that Kate has come to better understand and to trust Kilee, she too has developed a loving protectiveness over her. As she once told me, "Mom, I know it's weird, because Kilee is so much bigger and older than me, but I think of her as my little sister."

When my children play with Kilee, they play her way, which means they scream with uncensored delight when playing Jenga and the tower of wooden blocks they are attempting to build comes crashing down. Kilee, Kate and Tygre love music and often dance together in the living room. They also both take singing lessons, learning some of the same songs so that they can sing together at home. Kate helps Kilee colour and paint, and both she and William walk the dog with her and take her on ski runs.

Kilee had a Valentine's Day party for all five girls in her

special-needs dance class this year. Kate led the dancing while William DJed. Neither of them balked at being asked to play ABBA's "Dancing Queen" again and again and again. When one of Kilee's guests twirled so long and so hard that she banged into William, he just smiled, then moved on to the next song, "I'm a Gummy Bear." Seeing my two teenagers completely comfortable with Kilee and her friends was heart-warming. Kate good-humouredly recounted all the amusing things that happened, and William shared with me Kilee's excitement over having so much fun. He even suggested that Kilee have a Christmas party this year.

I've had friends ask if I ever thought twice about being with Patch, since it also meant taking on Kilee. That question surprises me. Patch is a package deal, all of him—his life, his dreams, his history. So am I. In being with me, he has to love all of me, not just the soft cuddly bits but the edgy bits, the moods I still struggle to work through, the sadness that sometimes overtakes me. Both Patch and I bought into the whole package when we decided to live together. Some parts of our life are hard, but more of it is simply wonderful, and at its centre is a burning love that's hard to put into words, a love so deep that it sometimes catches me unawares, taking my breath away. Even when I am spitting bullets because I am so angry with something he did or an assumption he made, I can look past that to see the man and how much I love him.

Watching Patch with Kilee stirs my heart; it's like watching my own babies grow—the tenderness with which he brushes her hair, or laces her shoes, or kisses her on the cheek. He has endless patience for her repeated words, her never-ending requests for her dinosaurs, a peach, an apple.

Patch's brother, Eddie, tells of one Christmas, years ago, when Kilee ran downstairs during the excitement of opening presents. They found her in the basement in a sea of washing detergent, bleach, fabric softener and Windex, having emptied every single container in the cleaning closet onto the floor. Patch just looked at Kilee, sighed deeply and said, "Ah, buddy, why did you have to go and do that?"

I see a version of that kind of forbearance replayed in so many ways: when Patch gets up early on the weekend to make Kilee's breakfast and clean her soiled sheets; when he teaches her to keep her skis together as she goes down a hill; when he reads the same story to her again and again; when he helps her say her prayers each night, prompting her with "Gr" for "Grandma," "Mmm" for "Mommy," "Ty" for "Tygre." Every evening it's the same prayer, and every evening he works through it with her, name after name, word after word. Because I've been in Kilee's life for only a few years, I'm happy for her to rhyme off those people she's known longer in an assured chorus, without change or interruption.

I often wonder how different Patch would be if Kilee hadn't come into his life. I wonder if he'd have the same humility, the same compassion. Patch once told me that having Kilee made him feel helpless for the first time as an adult. He would sit in the playroom with his baby girl, watching as she bit her hand or banged her head, refusing to meet his eyes. He yearned in every fibre of his being to make contact with her, but he just couldn't make it happen. His will seemed puny against the force of her isolation and the intensity burning inside her. For part of each day, he'd try to enter her world, to build up enough love and acceptance that she would trust him enough to let him in. That very first time those huge blue eyes finally looked right at him in recognition, he experienced complete elation, sending an electric shock of hope through his entire body.

While life with Kilee can be trying, it is also remarkable. I become so excited when she is able to tell me a story of something that has happened to her. The other day she not only remembered going to Island View Beach with her caregiver but was also able to access the language to tell me about it. "It was hot," she said with conviction.

Nothing I have done in my life has taught me as much humility as helping raise Kilee has. Each day, she pushes and challenges me in ways that are so different from those I face with William and Kate. Most of all, I am asked to find and to open up the tenderest place in my heart in order to accept whatever happens in the time we are together. Not to judge, not to expect, not to control. Yet every time I read an article about autism, the questions start up: *Is this a technique we could try with Kilee? Would a drug help? Will this type of therapy encourage language skills? Should we hire a speech therapist to work with Kilee every day? Are we being too demanding, or maybe not demanding enough?* The questions go on and on— questions without definitive answers. When Kilee's caregivers turn to us for advice about her behaviour, much of the time our answer is "I don't know." Whenever Patch gave me that non-answer early in our relationship, I would feel frustrated and slightly angry: *This is your child we're talking about here. How could you not know?* Over time, I realized that it's about the most honest answer he could give. When it comes to Kilee, much of the time we just don't know.

Some days I wonder if I'm good enough for the job, but that kind of attitude is a luxury, since parents don't have a choice. Patch is very considerate about not pushing Kilee on me, letting me choose to spend time with her rather than seeing me as a convenient babysitter. I appreciate his respect for me, but I also feel a tremendous responsibility for Kilee, along with a desire to contribute positively to her life. At the same time, I know this can happen only if I also give myself enough space to invest in self-care. When I'm rundown and hard-pressed I cannot truly give of myself to Kilee and be present for her.

I also confess that sometimes when I look at this kid, I marvel at all the human effort it takes to keep her healthy and functioning in our home. I wonder if we are doing the best for her, even though Patch's financial means allow us to employ an army to help her live the highest-quality life she can. Most other special-needs children I have met have one parent who stays home with them, eventually becoming a best friend and full-time advocate. I wonder if Patch and I, with our big sprawling lives, are providing the routine and predictability she needs, despite our love and best intentions.

Kilee's day begins with a morning nanny, who wakes her up, then takes her urine-soaked sheets down to the laundry room. Once back upstairs, she measures out the right amount of shampoo and conditioner for Kilee so that she won't squeeze the entire contents of both bottles down the drain. At the same time, she must watch to see that Kilee doesn't pull down the shower curtain, or throw all the dry towels into the water, or engage in any number of other unpredictable behaviours.

Kilee's no-sugar, low-carb diet requires extensive preparation, so her morning nanny leaves Kilee to finish showering and busily chops vegetables and fries chicken while Patch and I help the other kids with their breakfasts, sign notices for school or engage in a last-minute search for Kate's shoes—all the time hoping Kilee won't get into trouble up in the bathroom. Once Kilee comes down to the kitchen, if we are not there we need her two caregivers on duty at all times, in case she suddenly attempts to empty the refrigerator, drops a jar of pickles on the floor or throws the butter dish.

Kilee must be driven to school. A teacher meets her at the door, and for the rest of the school day she is within an arm's reach of two teachers. Back at home, a therapist works with her for several hours each day.

After school sometimes, Kilee's dad, often with an assistant, takes her swimming with yet another teacher. The pool has been the scene of some of Kilee's most dramatic meltdowns. On one occasion, when the fridge in the teen's social room was left unlocked, Kilee grabbed a tray of cupcakes and began stuffing them in her mouth so quickly that she had eaten a couple before her caregiver could snatch them away. All that sugar, along with her caregiver's high anxiety, only increased Kilee's excitement—she raced around the room, laughing hysterically. When the caregiver, by some small miracle, manoeuvred her out of the cafeteria and into the quiet of the library, Kilee managed to find food there as well: spotting a chocolate bar in a librarian's office, she dove through the open door, grabbed the bar, then started ransacking the office. The caregiver, realizing she was out of her depth, asked the stunned library patrons to help, and one of the librarians had the presence of mind to call the police.

Eventually, Kilee calmed down enough to sit outside on

a bench. That was when she remembered the cafeteria. She dashed off, gained entry and began grabbing dishes of Jell-O and pudding, scaring the cafeteria staff so much that they shut the sliding metal doors to contain her.

That's when the police arrived. A policewoman, who happened to have a special-needs daughter, spoke calmly to Kilee while the other officers gently restrained her.

This was the first time the police had to be called to help with Kilee, and fortunately the episode ended peacefully. Our fear had been that if ever we needed them, they might come with guns drawn. I've since heard that several police jurisdictions across Canada have been developing a database in which caregivers can register their autistic loved ones, which is reassuring. Nevertheless, this incident served as a warning that anyone who works with Kilee must always remain on high alert and never underestimate what can happen, especially in a public place.

So there it is: one child with so many caregivers, along with a massage therapist, pediatricians, naturopaths and playroom therapists. The team of people supporting Kilee is enormous, and yet all of us still get burned out. In the last six months, four people on Kilee's team have quit because of her outbursts, her dives for food, her screaming and grabbing, which seem to come out of nowhere. For a few weeks, we think we're doing well, then things turn very, very bad. It's hard on Patch, this constant failure.

I so often wish that Kilee could enjoy the normal pleasures that most of us take for granted, like having friends her own age to love and share and care about. For a special-needs child, this is a huge challenge. Kilee has never been invited to a birthday party or on a play date with a child her own age. Her unpredictable behaviour has left a scary impression on almost every classroom or sports team or group activity in which she has participated. And then there is her lack of language skills. When a person has trouble responding to questions, let alone initiating conversation, that's a pretty big bridge to cross. Yet the Kilee I have come to know has a sweetness and enthusiasm for life that makes her easy to love. The smallest things delight her—a handful of craft beads, the music on her iPod. Few other teenagers are willing to express their joy and affection as openly as Kilee.

When Kate's, William's or Tygre's friends come to our house, Kilee lights up by laughing or blushing with excitement. This signalled to Patch and me that she would like to socialize with kids her own age. Teenagers naturally want to hang out with other teenagers and to show their independence. They're also conscious of their appearance. For a family dinner out this summer, Kilee borrowed a pair of Kate's shoes that had a slight heel—a first for Kilee. It was fun to see her walk, ever so carefully, in the sleek black party shoes. They were a bit too small for her, but when we suggested she take them off for the ride home, she adamantly shook her head no.

As our other three kids become more involved with sleepovers and weekend parties, the gap between the kind of life Kilee leads and the life of a neurologically normal child grows much larger. When I first came into Kilee's life, I thought this was unique to her, but since then I've read that the isolation of any special-needs child becomes more profound as she grows older, because of an inability to understand friendships. I long for another teenager to love Kilee for who she is, to share her delight at bursting bubbles, at pouring paint out of its container, over and over and over again. I long for Kilee to have a friend who isn't afraid when she has a tantrum or suddenly bites her own hand and stomps her feet. I long for her to have one of life's greatest joys—real friendship with an affectionate give-and-take that is lasting and aware.

It is only recently that Patch has been able to start talking with me about Kilee's future; it has the potential to hold outcomes of which he is deathly afraid, like group homes that won't meet her needs, medication that spaces her out and the strong possibility that she will always need twenty-four-hour care.

Kilee can't cross the street on her own, but we continue to hope that one day she could live somewhat independently, and also find someone to love her. Whether these dreams come true seems less important than the inspiration they provide, because dreams push us to try new things, to believe in our children and to not be limited by a diagnosis. Dreaming doesn't mean we're oblivious to realities. I like to term this approach "realistic optimism," and to believe that many challenges are surmountable.

While our goals for Kilee must be different from those we hold for our other kids, they have the same foundational principles. We want all four to have safe, happy, rewarding lives; meaningful work; a sense of community; and the chance to make a difference in the world. We believe all these are possible for Kilee. Her work may be folding towels two hours a day or unloading a dishwasher. Her community may be a group home or an apartment with a caregiver who takes her on regular outings. Despite having to rely on others to help her shower, clothe her and feed her, Kilee already makes a difference beyond that of most children by teaching the rest of us about acceptance, about specialness, about compassion.

Patch has a library of books on autism. He has also taken hundreds of hours of training to be a better teacher and parent for Kilee. When he speaks to his team of ten thousand employees about the three As in his life—arthritis, accident and autism—he describes autism, not the almost crippling rheumatoid arthritis he has had since he was thirty-two, as the biggest challenge.

In Patch's first book, *Living the Good Life*, he embraced the adage "Good enough is good enough." When you have a special-needs child, it's especially important to be able to say, "I've done my best to care for and to create the best opportunities possible for this child. I can't be a perfect parent, only good enough."

Absorbing that isn't easy. My partner overcame great obstacles to create and control his enormously successful company. As an Olympic athlete, I certainly wasn't satisfied with "good enough." Every day I strove to surpass what was reasonable in my drive to become the best in the world.

When raising children, this goal of perfection is likely to drive you—and your kids—crazy. So much in parenting can't be foreseen or controlled, and maybe I had to be hit over the head twice with a two-by-four by having two children with special needs in order to understand this.

Patch and I are doing our best. We will never be able to anticipate everything, to recognize all our children's needs and to open every door. We can, however, approach each day with an open mind and an open heart, saying, "God gave this opportunity to me, along with my tasks for the day, so I think I'll give it a whirl."

* * *

Lately, I've begun to wonder if some of my concerns and wishes for Kilee are merely projections of what I believe she *should* have, rather than what she needs and indeed wants. When I observe her isolation from her peers, I don't always reflect on the many positive interactions she does have. One girl at school chooses to come to Kilee's classroom each week to read magazines with her. Megan, an adult friend who's known Kilee since she was born, takes her for walks, to her home for dinner and to the park to play. Then there are the other special-needs girls in Kilee's weekly dance class, who hold her hand as she enters the circle, led by the beautiful energy of their teacher, Tracy. These teenagers know Kilee, they dance with her, they join her when she laughs and they look at her quizzically or ask what's wrong if she cries.

Kilee can't tell us in words how she feels, or what she dreams about or what she hopes for herself, but I find that I learn more about her inner world, and I become more optimistic, when I observe her rather than project my own feelings onto her.

Every June, Operation Trackshoes provides youth with intellectual disabilities an opportunity to enjoy a weekend of athletic and social events in a community of people who embrace them without judgment. When Kilee came home with her dad after the Saturday sports competitions, she proudly showed me her nine ribbons. All were blue, so

I assumed she must have won every event she entered. As a competitive athlete, I was naturally interested in how fast she had run and how high she had jumped. Apparently in the 50-metre race, Kilee had dashed out ahead of the pack and was leading until she stopped to wave at her competitors. After that, she ran backwards for a while, finishing only when her dad came out on the course to run beside her. The high jump was Kilee's favourite, but instead of jumping over the bar, she found it more fun to run under it at full speed, then leap onto the nice cushy crash mat. After each event, all the participants were allowed to choose the colour of ribbon they wanted. Kilee happened to like blue a lot.

I asked Patch why he hadn't coached Kilee to jump over the bar rather than letting her run under it. I also wondered why he hadn't entered her in the afternoon swimming competition; her strength and technique would likely have won her a medal. When I told him I'd like to enrol Kilee in a competitive swim program, he agreed, while reminding me how difficult it is to keep her on the surface of the water—she likes to constantly dive to touch the bottom of the pool.

That same Saturday evening, Operation Trackshoes held a dance for its young competitors. All afternoon I'd been ferrying kids around the city to other events, and I knew I had to get up at six on Sunday morning for William's triathlon; however, I didn't want Kilee to miss her first chance to attend a teen dance, so I offered to drive her.

For the occasion, Kilee had chosen to wear a pretty flowered shirt with her favourite shorts. We arrived early so she could become comfortable in the noisy room full of kids and adults. I must admit that even I felt a little awkward, as most of them seemed to have bonded with a team during the afternoon.

When the DJ announced he was ready to start the music, a great cheer filled the room. And then something amazing happened. Every teenager—every single one—ran, wheeled and jumped onto the dance floor. The adults joined them, so that every seat in the room was empty, and everyone was dancing, singing and jumping around. The first dance was to ABBA's "Dancing Queen," Kilee's favourite song. She flung up her arms and squealed, and I overflowed with all the love and energy I felt around me. I have never experienced anything like it. There wasn't an ounce of self-consciousness in the room. Parents boogied with the kids; the twins Scott and Neil, who have Down's syndrome, were among the coolest and most happening as they did the fish, the wave, the lawnmower, the sprinkler, both with huge smiles. My heart grew two sizes, and I started crying.

Two dances in, a young man who had joined our little dance group started spinning. Kilee was the only person I'd ever seen do this, and I was delighted to discover that this was actually a hip dance move. After watching him in astonishment for a few seconds, Kilee jumped over beside him to launch her own high-speed spinning.

That was when everything came together for me and I finally got it. The whole day had nothing to do with who was the best athlete, or who was autistic or had Down's syndrome. This was about joy, pure and simple. The organizers of Operation Trackshoes offered an opportunity for those with intellectual disabilities to play and run and jump and dance and connect with a community of people who embraced them without judgment. These teens and adults live every day in a world where they don't fit in, not because of anything they are doing wrong but because of others' discomfort with those who look, act and speak differently. Yet they possess a real gift, the gift of expressing themselves authentically, without the self-censorship that sifts out so much joy. We're the ones who are disabled in our lack of ability to risk letting go because of our deep-rooted attachment to being like everyone else. For proof, we need only look at TV shows and magazine ads reflecting our desire to appear and act according to some invented social ideal, which is trotted out as the norm and erodes our individuality, originality and creativity.

On that particular Saturday night, I couldn't help but wonder how often our fear of being too conspicuous prevents us from experiencing joy. These kids aren't ever going to be the ones straightening their hair, getting their teeth whitened and wearing expensive designer jeans. They will never fit into society's idea of normal because they redirect the energy we spend on conformity into expressing love, joy and happiness.

When yours is a special-needs child, you and that child stand out the minute you walk into a bookstore or coffee shop, but before long, you stop caring. You know you have been chosen to travel a special journey with your child. However difficult it may be, you know it's the journey of a lifetime.

That day I stopped complaining about lost swimsuits and too many hours spent driving the kids around. That day, through Kilee, I remembered that every experience contains the potential for joy, if we just get up when the music begins and start dancing.

Kilee, our special-needs child, is teaching all of us.

Part V

TAKING STOCK

REAR-VIEW MIRROR

A few years ago, I invited my mom to meet me in Tampa, Florida, where I was making a presentation. She lived only a two-hour drive away, and I thought that we could visit for a few days. She got the date wrong and arrived while I was still en route. When she couldn't gain immediate access to the hotel room, she made such a scene that the event manager had to be called to calm her down and accommodate her. She sent angry messages to me, accusing me of standing her up.

It stressed me that my client had to deal with this, but then the situation only worsened. I had asked my mom to wait in our hotel room until after my event, when we could have dinner together. Instead, she turned up at the presentation, then invited herself to the reception. It was my middle-school graduation all over again. She told one woman she was wearing a colour that didn't flatter her—a favourite comment of my mom's. When another women exclaimed, "Your daughter is so wonderful!" my mom replied, "Oh, you don't know the whole story. Silken is no saint."

I overhead that one and steered her away from the woman.

The standing ovation I received for my presentation satisfied my client that I had done a good job; nonetheless, I was never invited to work with her again. I tried to tell myself this was no big deal—but the experience really shook me because my mom had penetrated into a part of my life that I had kept separate from her for two decades. Now, suddenly, here she was inside my safe bubble.

After my childhood wounds had begun to heal, I dreamed of having conversations with my parents in which the three of us acknowledged what had happened in the past and forgave one another. I thought at least they would notice how much I had changed, recognize my new-found peace and want to know something about my journey. This was a fantasy. Just because the lens through which I viewed the world had radically changed, it didn't mean that my dad would suddenly understand how much I once had needed his support, or that I would feel safe opening up to my mom about how overwhelmed I sometimes feel helping to raise four kids.

It's taken years for me to realize that my parents' journeys are different from mine—that they both have experienced incredible challenges in their lives, and that they have developed their own mechanisms for dealing with these hurts and losses.

In the fall of 1989, my mom married Janis, a retired employee of the Parks and Recreation Department of Cape Coral, based near Fort Myers, Florida, where they'd lived for a number of years. Their modest stucco bungalow is typical of the area except for one notable feature: as you approach, you see dry lawn, dry lawn, dry lawn—and then a wonderful oasis of orange and grapefruit trees. That's my mom's touch.

A minister conducted the marriage ceremony in this tropical orchard, with only my sister and me in attendance. My mom wore a short white lace dress that she'd made, and a small veiled hat.

My sister and I took the newlyweds out for dinner after their simple ceremony. They seemed happy, which made me happy for them, but for the most part I felt emotionally removed.

I know my mom chose to leave our family because her emotional state made any other course of action impossible for her. She feels safe and content in her twenty-four-year marriage, reinforcing her idea that all previous problems were someone else's fault. At seventy-four, after three hip replacements, Mom still buys the groceries and waters her big garden as part of her insistence on keeping busy. She does need help with the housework, but no one she hires will stay for long. After she accused the last helper of stealing and breaking her things, I asked, "Mom, do you think this might have something to do with you?"

"Now don't even start that!" she said dismissively—and in keeping with her habit of never looking back.

I have no idea what goes on in my mom's mind. I can't imagine how she perceives herself or her actions, but it's not normal for someone to be convinced that the neighbours are watching her, or that the man down the street secretly works for the government, or that the phone solicitor is really looking for information about your German heritage. These suspicions continue to leave her terribly isolated. My dad's response has always been "Ah, she's just Mom." He supported her for so many years that I have no doubt he loved her deeply. Her beauty, her radiance, her zaniness could be intoxicating, and it's hard to stay mad at someone who's nasty one minute, then smiling at you the next, making you think you were mistaken about the meanness.

My mom is more of a contradiction than anybody I know. Despite her dark moods, she can be one of the most enthusiastic and joyful people. Because of her years spent sculpting in hard stone with chisels and compressors, she has painful arthritis in her fingers, elbows and wrists, yet she continues to work in clay and has a kiln in her garage. She is always looking for ideas and is still highly creative. I can be buoyed by her delight when I invite her out for a beer and a bratwurst on a hot summer day. When I visit her, she moves into a flurry of planning with such gusto that even I can become convinced that we might have a good time together. And we do, for moments, for an hour, but darkness always lurks just below the surface—the harsh criticism, the cutting words and the jealousy.

It's hard to get a straight story from my mom. She talks two parts reality and eight parts fantasy, so that just when you think what she's telling you is based on facts, she puts an implausible spin on it or contradicts herself, causing you to dismiss the whole thing. She used to tell me that her dad made his living as a talented artist, which Oma later denied. She also told me that she came from a long line of musicians, which my cousin told me was untrue. These were small falsehoods, but they all contribute to the feeling that I can't take her at her word.

Even simple questions receive confusing answers. Before giving birth to William, I asked my mom about her pregnancy and labour in hopes of sharing this most primal and awesome of experiences. She proudly told me that she had weighed only 117 pounds on the day of the delivery, and that she gave birth to Daniele in three hours. My attempt to imagine my slender but hardly waif-like mother weighing only 117 pounds when pregnant was challenged further by her telling me that I weighed only six pounds at birth; the next day, she insisted it was eight pounds.

I feel guilty for not having a meaningful relationship with my mom. *What kind of daughter doesn't love and cherish her mother?* My mom conceived and carried me; she held me in her arms and she must have had hopes and dreams for me. My brother and sister both have a relationship with her. After visiting her a few months ago, Joerg told me that she seemed happier, and Daniele reported that she appeared to be mellowing with age. Summoning up my courage, I called Mom, inviting her for a visit and feeling happy that maybe we both had changed enough that everything would be okay. We even discussed our mutual need for physical space, appreciating that it might be best for both of us if she stayed in Patch's and my guest apartment, or maybe even a hotel.

Cheered by this success, I sent my mom an email about the kids, then even more bravely followed this with a picture of me on stage at a recent event. The next morning I received an email with multiple question marks in the subject line, asking "What in this world made you wear this terrible dress?"

This is what communication with my mom is sometimes like. This one was especially hurtful because throughout my childhood my mother had favourably compared her own petite frame to those of her daughters. Often she told us that what we were wearing looked ugly on us, and when she did compliment one of us, we nonetheless felt that, in her eyes, we would never be as beautiful or slim as she had been. I recognize that when these old hurts surface, it's unresolved emotions at work, but I couldn't pretend that such a comment was harmless. I emailed my mom, telling her that if we were going to rebuild our relationship, we had to establish some boundaries to protect not only me but also my children and stepchildren from abusive comments. I used those strong words purposefully: I wanted her to understand that her comments could cause damage.

My mom replied in a rampage, finishing her email by noting that she wondered what had happened to the happy, gentle Silken we all loved.

The Silken she was remembering isn't a Silken I remember. I remember the little girl who thought that she must deserve the insults hurled her way, the girl who developed such deep self-loathing that she wanted to punish herself every time she didn't perform perfectly. I'm so glad that my mom's hurtful comments no longer have the power to drive me to starve myself, or cut myself, or run eighteen kilometres. I am so grateful I finally discovered that I'm beautiful without being rail-thin, without needing to change the way I dress or speak or walk. My love for myself also tells me that I don't need to bring my mom into my life—for me, being healthy means not having negative relationships. That's the crux of it: the only relationship I will accept with her is a positive one.

When I read my mom's emails, it feels clear to me that she must suffer from all the negative thoughts inside her head. I wish she would seek help to gain insight into the events in her past that might have damaged her, but my gut feeling is that she won't. I can feel empathy, and I do love her. But I'm not made of stone and her comments do have the power to hurt me. Some part of me still nags me into believing that if my sister and brother can have a relationship with her, then I should be able to as well. We all have different bumps and bruises. It feels wrong to turn my back on her, but whenever I try to start afresh, it's not long before I'm wounded again. I used to let her comments float by unchallenged, but now I realize that I am dishonouring myself if I don't set limits.

I believe that my mom tries to love all her children and to love herself. My past remains part of my present, the same way hers does, and sometimes I still phone her just to hear her voice. I chat about this and that, and then I do something odd. I tell her about how slender I have become, or how good I look in the pretty dress I bought, trying out these dangerous comments, wanting her to tell me something nice—that I am beautiful, that I am smart and kind and funny. Futile as this may be, I yearn to have her tell me all the things I tell my daughter every day. I think of how Kate loves to crawl into bed beside me each night to read together in the final minutes of the day, feeling relaxed as we lie side by side, soaking up the attention, wanting me to read one more page, then wanting to tell me one more story about her day. I still yearn for this from my mom—to experience what my daughter has from me. Sometimes I am overcome by the feeling of this missing, a primal feeling that descends into my chest and quickens my breath. I long to feel my mom's arms holding me, to feel safe in her presence, to know the fun of making cookies together or going shopping. I want this unconditional love of a mother for a child that I know I will never get. This longing is so unconscious that it startles me when it arises. *How can I miss something so deep and personal that I never experienced? How can I miss someone who never existed?*

Of course, after yet another disappointment, I hang up the phone, feeling dissatisfied and angry—angry mostly at myself because I know that despite all the work I've done, my mom still has the power to reduce me to a hopeful puppy dog looking for affection. Once again I must remind myself that she can no more give me what I want than she can change the past or predict the future. She cannot make me feel how I, as her child, want to feel. It's now my job, as an adult, to take responsibility for feeling loved and treasured.

My first reaction when I found out I was pregnant with William was joy. My second was terror. *What if I become my mom?* I've often heard friends joke about hearing their mother's voice in their own when they scold their children. For me, that was no joke. Every time I acted irrationally around my children, or raised my voice too sharply, or yelled over their yelling, I wondered if that dreaded transformation was taking place. In my early parenting days, the persistent fear that I would screw up was like a fog that tempered the normal mother–baby joys. It was the thought torturing me when I banged my head against the hallway wall, my children locked in our hotel room, and when, in a fury, I threw a plate against William's bedroom wall—my mom's signature response to frustration.

Neil warned me that the surest way to become my mom was to try too hard not to become my mom. In other words, the fear and anxiety that I experienced trying *not* to be irrational, unpredictable and explosive actually could make me irrational, unpredictable and explosive. Even now, when I think that I am acting like my mom, my inner world becomes a horrifying place. I chide myself for being a bad person and for the sharpness in my voice. It's when I'm stressed that this happens, because stress is synonymous with that nasty voice that berates me for being unkind, that tells me I'm horrible to live with and that asks who would want to be my partner, let alone my friend?

My mom watched me row at the 1996 Olympics in Atlanta, Georgia, my last race before retiring and one in which I won silver. I never especially wanted her present. She always claimed that rowing had made me hard. In fact, it was surviving her wrath that made me hard enough to compete in the Olympic arena.

We all love happy endings, in which people are reconciled, love is realized and everyone lives happily ever after. For years, I yearned for all the loose threads of our relationship to be neatly tied. I am still yearning.

* * *

Returning home to my dad's house in Mississauga, where I lived for most of a decade, is both an uplifting and an unsettling experience. I am excited to see my dad—I love him dearly, and he is fun to be around—yet so much of my past is buried in the walls of that house that old feelings of anxiety return, along with a hypervigilance that keeps me on edge, waiting for the visit to fall apart.

Going home again, I am eight and twenty-one and forty-eight all at the same time. I feel powerless all over again. I'm careful with what I share about my life, and so I sometimes push my dad away. Sometimes he'll repeat his old mantras—that my childhood was good and normal—and I know I need to hold on to my own truth and know that I'm not crazy or misremembering. And so I come home to my dad with my arms open but ready to shield myself, because I have been forced, too much, too often, to shore up my dad's survival mechanisms. I forgive him, while maintaining my clarity and strength. I know what my experience was, and I know how much it has cost me to heal.

At age seventy-five, my dad is still physically robust at the same time as he is becoming psychologically and emotionally older. He was never the best listener, but now he physically can't hear, so that much of our conversation suffers from the broken-telephone effect. He misses pieces of dialogue, starts talking when somebody is in mid-sentence and fails to answer questions.

Last summer, we had a family reunion at a fishing lodge Patch owns in Quebec. Along with my dad, there was Joerg with his wife and two kids; Daniele and David, with their daughter; and all of Patch's and my gang—Tygre and Kilee, with her nanny, Violetta; William and Kate; and our dogs, Bliss and Balto. We were supposed to be staying from Wednesday to Sunday, but after two days, Dad decided he wanted to leave. He felt left out of the activity around him, but at the same time he was convinced that all of us were talking about him and deciding he wasn't totally with it—an old paranoia that someone is conspiring against him still sometimes creeps back. I hate that his hearing problem leaves him feeling iso-lated, but he resists my pressure to wear his hearing aid. I just want him to feel like the beloved Opa he is in the company of his grandchildren.

My dad is a wonderful guy who, because he's been through so much, is uncomfortable with confronting his feelings. When he's out of his element, the old repressed emotional problems—the anger, the injustices and the insecurities—start surfacing. I fear his Laumann stubbornness will stop him from making a truce with becoming older, preventing him from reaching out to counsellors, friends and family who could help him with these natural anxieties.

That day at the fishing lodge, Dad wanted to get away as fast as possible, to return to an environment where every-thing was familiar and revolved around him. Being isolated in a setting that he didn't own must have felt like an emergency to him. He was also missing his wife, Laura.

My dad and Laura were married in 1990 in a civil cere-mony at City Hall, followed by a party in Dad's backyard. It was a nice wedding, the whole event imbued with the sense of ease that is often characteristic of a second wedding. My dad and Laura are crazy about each other. She has styled him up, and when they're together, they're always holding hands or touching. Laura makes him happy, and I am so grateful he has a partner to grow old with.

Every family goes through adjustments as parents age, but because I have refused to truly acknowledge that my once-all-powerful dad is failing, it shocks me when he acts old. It's obvious to everyone that he is quite deaf, but he gets angry if we talk loudly to accommodate him, and he hates his hearing aid. I know that I have inherited both my dad's hearing problems and his stubbornness. Already I am losing the low tones, so that if people mumble or drop their voices, I miss what they're saying. It's incredibly frustrating to be straining to hear, yet I won't go get tested. I'm learning a bit of what my dad is going through—and also that I shouldn't be hard on him, as William and Kate will probably soon be frustrated with me in the same way.

All this saddens me, since I am crazy about my dad. He is intelligent and driven, never losing his motivation to build his business, which has just celebrated its fortieth anniversary, or to create a terrific life for his kids and now Laura. Even today, he helps my brother make financial decisions, and serves as the foundation for our family. While I was growing up, I saw my dad as larger than life—Dad, the power piece to the family. With his strong personality and his big temper, he was an imposing figure to all of us. When I recently mentioned to my dad that Mom and I weren't getting along, he once again attempted to convince me: "Silken, it wasn't really that bad." *Not bad, all those nights of terror?* He continued by saying how the end of his marriage was mostly his fault: "I worked all the time. I never called to say I'd be late. I didn't understand how to communicate." Then he told me that since Mom is getting older and more set in her ways, maybe I should just accept her as she is. I told him that I refused to let anyone treat me badly, including Mom, and that if that was the price, then I wouldn't spend time with her. I felt like screaming because here it was all over again, the reason I'm tense, why I'm hypervigilant. No one, not even Dad, can tell me what my experience was or what kind of relationship I should have. When I balk, he shrugs his shoulders as if to say that I'm being irrational, and then he comes back later to say the same things all over again, until I shrug my shoulders to indicate that, to me, it's him who is acting irrationally.

I understand the need to control, but the idea that anyone can control one's own life, let alone the lives of others, is an illusion. Not only do our efforts fail to protect us but they can also drive us mad as we race around performing tricks trying to preserve that illusion. Life is unpredictable. The desire to protect ourselves from change causes us to act out of our fears, our shames and our desires, instead of allowing us to see and respond to what actually is happening. Letting go of that attempt to control has been one of the most difficult and liberating experiences of my life. Healing for me has been about allowing the past to come forward so that it moves through me, rather than getting stuck inside me. It has been about softening the tight spots in my psyche, about loosening the muscular grip of my past on my present.

My dad's insistence on control often reveals itself in his intensely competitive nature. One day when he and William were playing air hockey, he worked himself into a frenzy because my son was messing with the rules of the game. Finally, my dad threatened to quit in a huff if William wouldn't stop—Dad didn't want to lose. It's funny how clearly I can see the intensity of his competitive nature while having trouble recognizing the same streak in myself. When I was an athlete, I wanted to achieve my potential in something I loved, but I didn't realize how much I also detested being beaten.

So, yes, I understand the competitive drive that had my dad complaining when his grandson was messing with the

rules. I believe I've also inherited the flip side of that quality—my dad's playfulness, which can be incredibly endearing.
He is not afraid to be silly; even as I write this, here in my
office in Victoria, I can hear him hooting and hollering as he
plays a killer game of badminton with William. This time it's
Opa who is fooling around, trying to hit the birdie backwards
while hopping on one foot. They are also talking big, trying to
psyche each other out. It's times like this when my kids adore
being with their opa. I wish he had more of these moments.
But my dad doesn't like breaking his routine and so loves to
have us visit him but is reluctant to come to us.

I see my dad's vulnerability, in which his hearing loss
plays a defining role. I also see parts of myself in Dad, and I
wish he could find the peace that I have found by spending so
much time naming and defanging the demons that were bent
on torturing me.

★　★　★

I suppose every family has its stories about each member's
identity. Parents begin the family group with a sense of themselves and how they perceive each other. Then, as each child
is added, he or she is defined by the others, and especially by
the parents. One kid may be seen as casual and easygoing,
another as rebellious, a third as practical and ambitious.

Just as I am learning to free myself from the voices of the
past that sought to define me, so I need to create a new, more
accurate image of my siblings, free of family stereotyping. I
am embarrassed to say it was only a few years ago that I really
began to build relationships with Daniele and Joerg not just as

"my big sister" and "my little brother" but as the people they really are. It's been exhilarating and liberating.

As the oldest in the family, Daniele was bombarded the most with projections of who she was, especially by our mother, whose jealous accusations interfered even with my sister's ability to study. Sadly, for a long time, my view of Daniele was tainted by my mom's characterization of her as clumsy and conservative.

I wish now that I had the power to go back into the past and to comfort that little Daniele, who today seems so strong and rational and impenetrable. I wish I could let that little girl know how incredibly gifted and loving and kind she would turn out to be. When I think about the moments in our childhood where I repeated my mom's taunting words, glad that my tall, beautiful and accomplished sister was the object of her contempt and not me, I burn with shame, because Daniele has stood by me in the best and hardest moments of my life. She and her wonderful husband, David, have been there for me through the births of my children and my divorce, and they have cheered me through the building of my new life. She and I are mirror images of each other—her measured perspective grounds my highest highs and lowest lows, and I like to think that my boundless optimism helps her to push beyond the practical.

David, the United Church minister my sister married, is outgoing, smart and personable—the kind of guy who makes everyone feel good in his presence, yet who can still inspire you to think about life a little differently. Theirs was the wedding that I attended as maid of honour in North Bay, just before I was injured at the 1992 World Championships in Essen. The ceremony was held on a rock in the woods by the water, on a blanket Daniele had quilted. David sang to her a song he had written, accompanying himself with his guitar. It was wonderful to see my sister so happy.

*   *   *

My younger brother, Joerg, is the person in the family whose life story I know the least. He seemed isolated on his own little island in the house we shared, and afterward he slipped out of my life for a very long time while he played out his wild side in legendary adventures, sometimes deplorable and sometimes laudable. Occasionally, he would pop up in one city or another, and I know my dad rescued him on a number of occasions, creating a strong bond between them. Irresponsible in his youth, Joerg is now a splendid father of two. He runs our dad's business, and he's a good and loyal friend whom I'm enjoying getting to know.

Joerg is the softest of all of us, and his gentleness and compassion shine through when you meet him. I am so grateful that his focus on his own family has brought us together again. When Joerg asked me why I always suggested seeing him and his wife at our dad's house, rather than visiting them directly, I realized that I still saw my dad as the focal point for our family, which distracted me from developing an independent relationship with my brother and his family. Joerg always has that ability to see things so clearly and to speak directly from the heart. It's been a wonderful surprise for this older sister to find that her little brother has grown into an incredible source of wisdom.

*   *   *

My love for my siblings is fierce. We have a deep connection to one another and a loyalty that has withstood time and distance. As in every family, conflicts, misunderstandings and dramas happen from time to time, but none of this seems to matter. If I become frustrated by something my sister or brother has done, I take a step back and think of all we've been through, and how it has shaped each of us in different ways. We've had enough pain, enough divisiveness, enough self-doubt, enough silence. Now it's time for healing.

OLYMPIC FEVER

On Friday, October 30, 2009, I helped carry the Torch, in tandem with Olympic diver Alexandre Despatie, on its odyssey across Canada to the 2010 Winter Olympic and Paralympic Games in Vancouver. As torchbearers, we were passing inspiration from one generation to another, hand to hand, to realize the collective dream of excellence for our country. What we were also passing along was hope—hope that all the countries of the world could continue to work through their differences and their challenges to assure that humanity has what it takes not only to survive but to achieve global harmony.

That was a lot of expectation for the little Greek flame flowing through my hands. It's an ancient flame, travelling through the centuries and across thousands of kilometres to share its message. In the months leading up to the 2010 Olympics, I was one of twelve thousand Canadians running, wheeling, rowing and skiing it across the country, holding high that hope and inspiration for our few allotted minutes.

My biggest thrill in carrying the Torch as one of Canada's first runners (okay, walkers) was having my kids on the lawn of the BC legislature watching and cheering. Actually, screaming would be more accurate. Kate, hoisted on Patch's shoulders, was hollering, "Go, Mommy!" as if I were competing in an Olympic final. That didn't make me walk any faster. I just wanted to fully enjoy the thrill of carrying the flame and the energy of the crowd for my full two hundred metres.

After Vancouver won the right to hold the 2010 Olympic and Paralympic Games, William became over-the-top Olympics crazy. On the Friday that I carried the Torch, he clung to me like Velcro, which for a twelve-year-old boy was unexpectedly endearing. Only later did I realize that it wasn't me he was clinging to. It was the Torch.

"Can we mount it in my room?" he asked the moment I walked through our front door. "It's our torch, right, Mommy? Can I take it to school on Monday?"

My daughter wanted this wonderful show-and-tell piece, too, but my son made his position clear: "Shotty on the Torch!"—meaning, *I called it.*

I was left to wonder, *Could the inspirational stuff I've always believed about the Olympics already be working on my son? Is this a passing phase, or does he have a serious, life-affecting Olympic fever?*

What I know for sure is that thousands of Canadians were moved to tears by carrying, or simply cheering on, the Torch. I saw the sparkle in the eyes of our young rowers as they received it from their heroes, the gold-medal men's eight. I saw the poignant expression of a woman who was carrying the Torch for a husband who had never been able to run because of polio. I spoke to random spectators, each one moved like thousands of other Canadians into a very public display of national pride. What that little flame represented was beyond the power of words. What I was witnessing that day was the magic of the Torch.

The Olympics are also big business. Sponsors, media, government, sport governing bodies—all have a vested interest in the Games. This means they're controlled by too few people with too much power, making it difficult to shake up the closed circuit that the Olympics as an institution have become. At their core, though, the Games are something positive and powerful. They're about dreams and possibilities. They're about young people who have the courage to train for staggering amounts of time, and then to put it all out there in one big, mind-blowing, heart-thumping effort. They're about kids who one day were inspired by something they saw or heard or experienced and said, "I want to do that." Then, through pluck, and perhaps some luck, they began to practise and to achieve until they found others willing to believe in them, to support their dreams, to guide them. Soon they were consumed by their ambition to become the best in the world at their chosen sport. Perhaps it was something popular, like ski jumping. Perhaps it was as little known as skeleton, where you slide headfirst down a frozen track, or women's rowing, or short-track speed skating.

The Olympics provide an opportunity to pull all that training, all that focus, all those dreams together, to compete on an international stage beside the world's best athletes, all peaking at the same time, in the same full-out, nothing-in-reserve arena. To me, the Olympic spirit is epitomized by the willingness of an athlete, despite all that pressure, to put aside personal dreams of glory, all those hopes fuelled by a desire to win, for the greater good. I saw that in 1992, when Jenny Walinga bowed out of the women's fours and eights, just days before the finals, because she feared her back injury might cost her crews a medal. When Kay Worthington took her place in the four and the boat crossed the finish line in gold position, Jenny was on the sidelines cheering them on. Days later, without fuss or media attention, Brenda Taylor from the four presented to Jenny one of the two gold medals she'd won during the weekend's races. I witnessed this same generosity at the Winter Olympics in Salt Lake City, where the Canadian women's cross-country skiing team of Beckie Scott and Sara Renner was favoured to win. When Sara broke her pole in the final kilometre of the race, it was a Norwegian coach who handed her his athlete's spare. This is the spirit that I celebrate.

Two days before the Vancouver Olympics, my kids and I made a big banner echoing the slogan of these Games: "We Believe—In You." William wanted to hold it up at the Opening Ceremony for the athletes to see from the infield, causing me to realize something strange: though I had competed in four Olympics, I had never been to an Opening Ceremony. Not ever. When I was racing, I felt it would be too distracting when I needed to focus on winning. That was especially true in 1992, when I was asked to carry the flag—a once-in-a-lifetime thrill—but declined because I didn't see how I could handle the extra tension while trying to heal from my injury. I was right: I won my bronze by only a smidgen.

In Vancouver, my kids and I had the privilege of cheering on Clara Hughes as she carried Canada's flag. Clara is the only athlete in the world to win multiple medals in both the Summer and the Winter Games. In 2006, when she won a silver and her first gold, she scrawled the word "joy" on her hand. That was to honour everyone she'd met in Africa through Right To Play, an organization that uses sport to improve the lives of kids in impoverished countries. It was also to celebrate the joy and the deeper meaning that her participation in that organization had given to her. Clara donated her prize money to Right To Play, and through her challenge to Canadian companies, she raised another half million dollars.

After so many decades of men's sport dominating the media, it's encouraging to see more coverage of Canadian women, as well as of non-professional sport in general. When I spend time with our fabulous women's soccer team, or meet our gold-medal women's hockey team, it seems crazy to me that these superb athletes have so few professional opportunities while their male counterparts enjoy lucrative contracts.

I also hope that we will finally stomp to death the negative conversation about women's sports not being as competitive as men's. I hope we can move beyond comparing men's and women's times, the height of their jumps and the number of competitors in the field. All this is missing the point. When I'm watching the World Championship 800-metre final, I'm not thinking, *Boy, that Romanian woman is pretty slow compared with the men!* I'm thinking, *What a powerful runner! What a flawless strategy! What an incredible finishing kick!* Because women and men are different physically and mentally, we need to enjoy and celebrate each separately.

When Daniele and I won bronze in pairs in 1984 at Los Angeles, we were reaping the rewards of the courageous women rowers who had blazed a trail before us. These were the pioneers who had fought to have dedicated coaching time, boats that fit their bodies, uniforms that came in something other the men's sizes, the right to be included in the 1976 Summer Olympics, and then to be allowed to row a 2,000-metre course.

Women athletes still have inroads to make. Our ski jumpers were not allowed to compete in Vancouver despite their vigorous campaign. Last summer in London, Canada's five-time World Champion canoeist, Laurence Vincent-Lapointe, couldn't compete because there were no women's canoe events; the men had five. Only two members of our women's mountain-bike team—ranked the best in the world—could compete because the Olympic quota allowed for only 67 women, as opposed to 145 men.

It's true that high-level women's events generally do have fewer entries than the men's—a depressing reflection of how many countries don't support women competing at all, especially in sports considered unfeminine, such as rowing, wrestling and weightlifting. Historically, the women's eight has had to struggle to produce a full roster of international participants. Many countries filled out their eights by using their fours and pairs, though today few countries that participate are willing to risk doubling up in this way, as they want to win!

I'm always encouraged when I see a new country enter any event, but globally we are still a long way from realizing the right for women to enjoy physical activity. That's a shame; I believe sport is the single most powerful way of building positive body image, strength of character and a healthy self-concept. Many studies have shown that women who play sports are less likely to be sexually assaulted, less likely to become stuck in an abusive relationship, less likely to experience teenage pregnancy and more likely to go to college.

I believe that the International Olympic Committee, the IOC, must do more to promote gender equality. It was only when Human Rights Watch became involved that Saudi Arabia agreed to send two female athletes to London. That concession happened after international criticism had mounted high enough for Saudi Arabia to fear that the IOC might be pressured into barring its male athletes from competing. The precedent for this kind of sanction was established at the 1964 Olympics in Tokyo, when South Africa was banned because of its refusal to condemn apartheid.

Unfortunately, the 110-member IOC is dominated by men and old royal blood lines. I have heard IOC members proudly speak about how far women have come, but to be honest, I find it hard to see it. When you look at the few women in positions of influence, the predominance of men's events over women's, the miniscule number of nations that wholeheartedly support women in sport and the dismal investment in women's coaching, it's easy to feel discouraged. Last summer, as I listened to a CBC interview with Nikki Dryden, who is both a human rights activist and an Olympic swimmer, I was more forcefully struck by her arguments on how far women still have to go. The IOC must make it clear to all nations that inclusion in the Olympic Games means the inclusion of women as well as men. Sport is a place of empowerment, of encouraging women to believe anything is possible, which is why some governments fear it.

My daughter, Kate, recently discovered how unequal the world still is. Until last month, when she watched a movie at school about the status of women, it had never occurred to her that a gender difference in opportunity existed even in a country like Canada. She was incensed as she cited the number of women on corporate boards compared with men, the low number of women in top-level management, the hours that women still dedicate to their homes in comparison with their professional husbands. "Mom, the world is not fair!" she exclaimed. "With women not even having basic human rights in so many countries, I think it might be getting worse."

As I listened to my distraught and indignant daughter's compelling arguments, I realized I had become too accepting of the status quo. I'm currently on several boards, and listening to Kate now increased my commitment to pushing for stronger female representation. She also inspired me to devote more time to supporting young women through mentorship, and to more intentionally seek out audiences of women to inspire and encourage.

Part of the way I've tried to do that is through my work with Right To Play. At school Kate had been learning that the key to real change for women is educating girls, but my work with Johann Olav Koss has led me to believe that sport also has a huge role to play. As a Norwegian speed skater, Johann was an icon in the world of sport, having won four Olympic gold medals while also creating ten world records. After retiring from sport, he trained as a doctor at the University of Queensland in Australia, then earned a master's of business administration at the University of Toronto.

In July 2000, I received a note from Johann on the letter-head of Olympic Aid, an organization that helped the world's disadvantaged children. On a trip to Africa, he had been gal-vanized by the sight of children in refugee camps attempting to play soccer with a ball made of torn T-shirts. His response had been to fill a plane with sports equipment for those kids. Now, he was inviting me to accompany him to Africa to par-ticipate in a CBC documentary on Olympic Aid's work.

I had a lot of questions, including some that echoed those of Johann's critics: *Shouldn't food and water and health care be the first priority in a refugee camp? Wasn't sport a rather frivolous extra in a community struggling to meet basic human needs?*

Johann's challenge was a simple one: "Come with me to the Sudan and Eritrea to see for yourself."

Two weeks later, I found myself in the back of a white UN Refugee Agency vehicle blazing a dusty trail along the barely beaten road to the Lugufu Refugee Camp, in Tanzania. As we drew close, so many images of what such a camp looked like flashed through my mind, and soon I saw the tents of my imagination: brown and dusty, lined up one against another, many with small fires in front. Then I began to see the chil-dren—thousands of children, standing in groups outside the tents, some carrying younger children on their backs, or sit-ting listlessly inside the tents with their mothers. A parade of children followed our vehicle so that when we stepped out, we were totally surrounded.

The head of the camp introduced herself and other Olympic Aid workers, who then showed us around, the kids still fol-lowing us and laughing as they echoed our voices. I began to sing a silly song that I knew from having two kids under age four. The children sang back. Soon I was laying out my entire repertoire, to their delight. As Johann and the others chatted with the elders, I played with the kids, teaching them hopscotch, four square and duck, duck goose.

On our third day in Africa, the Olympic Aid coaches gathered the children for a soccer game, with me enlisted to encourage the girls. With their mothers clucking, "No, no, no," I urged them onto the field in a group, then threw a soccer ball into the air. The girls screamed as the ball flew up, then dropped at their feet. Most had never played with one before, but after the first few scary minutes of tossing one around, they acquired the knack, and they loved it.

After we demonstrated a few rules of the game, the Muslim girls tied back their headscarves in anticipation. A few minutes into the game, all the players were exuberant with joy, suddenly developing ball-handling skills that might have been the envy of many North American teams. After I came off the field, sweaty and exhausted, I was met by a UN worker overcome with emotion. When I enquired if anything was wrong, she replied, "You don't understand. Muslim girls playing with Christian girls? That just doesn't happen here!"

In that moment, I realized that the power of sport was far beyond anything I had imagined. That feeling was confirmed in Rwanda, where I watched Tutsi and Hutu children, whose tribes once tore each other apart in a vicious civil war, brought together by a red soccer ball and a field. Even in communities struggling for survival, play had the thrilling power to bridge religious and other cultural differences, to heal ancient resentments, to teach children and adults to respect one another.

In 2003, Johann created Right To Play, an international humanitarian organization that defines sport as a basic right of childhood, not just as a pleasant pastime. Its motto is profound but simple: Look After Yourself, Look After One Another.

Today, Right To Play operates in twenty-seven countries, using sport's transformative magic to educate and support children who face adversity on a daily basis. Through games, they build essential life skills and resilience, enabling even the most vulnerable to create better futures for themselves. They also drive social change in their communities in ways that have a lasting impact.

For the past decade, I have spent significant amounts of time volunteering in various capacities for Right To Play, including as a spokesperson and as the chair of the International Board of Directors. As a governance member on the board, I also visited Rwanda and Uganda to see first-hand how our projects were evolving.

Traditional ideas still dominate in many African villages, especially when it comes to acceptable behaviour for girls. In each new community, our enthusiastic young coaches work with our regional representatives to come up with a workable plan. Perhaps they'll suggest a soccer game—just a little game!—inviting the women from the village to participate. Sometimes it takes a lot of persuading, but they eventually agree because they trust our local representative. Many have never before touched a soccer ball, but within minutes they've lost their self-consciousness, and their enthusiastic shouts fill the air. Afterward they become the advocates for their daughters, insisting they must have the same opportunity to play.

I have witnessed whole villages change their attitude toward women through the introduction of sport for girls. Just as we see our own daughters gain confidence through success in sport, so those African mothers witness the transformation sport can bring, making them willing to stand up to ensure that it continues.

After sport—both for girls and for boys—has begun to flourish in one small village, then the next and the next, several villages may decide to hold a Right To Play tournament. This is where Johann's entrepreneurial and philanthropic genius combines with his medical experience. When the children are gathered for cooperative games, our Right To Play representatives teach them about HIV prevention, the importance of vaccines and the need to wash their hands before eating. It's been my observation that lessons learned through play are the sort children not only retain but also share with their parents.

It's these innovations that keep Right To Play exciting for those of us involved in its administration, as well as for those on the ground. I remember listening mesmerized as Dennis Bright, responsible for our West and Francophone Africa Region, addressed an International Board of Directors meeting. He spoke about growing up in Sierra Leone, where he absorbed his culture's restricted view of women, then described how his ideas had been transformed by his experience in government and with Right To Play. That caused me to reflect upon how differently I would have viewed my own future if I had grown up in a country like Sierra Leone. This education has made me redouble my sense of what is necessary for me to achieve with all my privileges.

I know that there's no easy fix for the myriad complex problems that face children in the world's trouble zones, but I also know first-hand the impact "just a little game" can have on them as they play together without thought of race or religion. These children will be the leaders who shape how their communities one day see and interact with the world. More play, better children, better citizens, better world.

★ ★ ★

Female athletes also face stereotypical attitudes about their competitiveness—a trait seen as admirable in men but not so much in women. Without a large dose of aggressiveness, no one can win in the Olympic arena. Every day in training you are pitting yourself against yourself, as well as against everyone else in the sport. Because of mixed messages, women sometimes handle their competitiveness less well than men. In my experience, when the male rowers got angry at one another, it was raw. They would curse, "You son of a bitch! You cut me off." Women are usually afraid to be that direct, so our repressed anger sometimes turns into deep-seated resentment. I know that some of the other women rowers were envious of all the media attention I received. With the guys, I didn't have to apologize for being good—but then, to be fair, I wasn't competing directly with them either.

Because of the old conflicted attitudes about female aggressiveness, I was slow to acknowledge how fiercely competitive I can be, and how this may have affected my relationships with other women rowers. At the very least, I credited myself with leaving my competitiveness "in the boat," even describing myself that way during speeches. I was surprised when my friends began joking that I was the most determined-to-win person they'd ever met. *Me?*

But it's true. I now know that I am ridiculously competitive. My kids and I can't even get through a game of Monopoly without someone crying because we're all so competitive. I love winning, and I always strive to be the best at everything, which is something that can take over my whole personality. Recently, I did a 100-kilometre Gran Fondo bike ride—which is the Tour de Victoria—supposedly just for the fun of it. For the first 10 kilometres I was content to ride with my friend, but when too many other cyclists started passing us, I began to speed up, and then to speed up again, until my friend was so far behind I couldn't see her. A better person would have waited, but instead I chased the pack ahead of me, and then the pack ahead of it.

Now that feedback has allowed me to know myself a lot better, I can sometimes step back to examine more objectively my motives and behaviour in various situations by asking myself, *Are you doing this because it's right for you, or just because you want to win?*

Before the 2000 Summer Olympics in Sydney, Australia, the CBC asked me to test as a commentator for the Games. Kate was less than a year old, and I wasn't sure I wanted to go away for six weeks, but I did the test anyway, and I received a callback. The choice, as I learned, had come down to me and Marnie McBean, with whom I'd always been competitive. *Hmm . . .*

All sorts of triggers about wanting to win were shooting off in my psyche. It was really hard for me to pull back and ask myself, *Is going to Australia really what I want to do?*

I decided it wasn't, so I didn't do the follow-up, which was the right decision for me.

On the other hand, a few years ago, I was invited by the mayor of nearby Oak Bay to be his challenger in the teacup boat race at the Oak Bay Tea Party. This lovely neighbourhood event has existed for fifty years. It boasts a fair, a small midway and a live band. The race consisted of the mayor and his notable challenger—in this case, me—navigating in tippy, oversized teacup-shaped boats (in which rowing skill did not necessarily determine success). Before I agreed, I asked if I could try the boat because I absolutely did not want to lose.

I was still nervous on the day of this little community party. When the race started, I jumped into one of the teacups and began rowing at thirty strokes a minute. In short order, I had raced around the buoy and was on my way back, while the mayor was still settling into his boat. The politically correct side of me kept saying, *Don't make the mayor look bad. Let him catch up a little.* The competitive side shouted, *Go, go!* And go I did.

To this day, he never seems thrilled to see me, but it's the absolute truth to say that I couldn't help myself. It's also true to say that I understand why people don't like those of us who are supercompetitive. We can be obnoxious, which is why I found it hard to accept that I am one of those crazies. Whether it's sculls or teacups, I get a laser-like focus that fuels me with an intensity that can be embarrassing. My only excuse for the teacup race was Olympic nostalgia: there I was, on the water, in a sort of boat with a paddle in my hands.

Which brings me back to Vancouver 2010.

Because I know how hard women have struggled to find some equality in sport, I found it so satisfying to hear Canada Hockey Place go crazy when the Canadian women's hockey team won gold. Canada's young hockey players are role models for all our girls, and at the 2010 Games, they pushed against many preconceived ideas of what it means to be athletic and feminine, blowing open the door on our national sport.

Fittingly, as I was leaving the arena, I encountered Mayor Hazel McCallion of Mississauga, who at ninety-two is one of the longest-standing elected leaders in North America. Smart, feisty, ambitious and a lifelong hockey fan, Mayor McCallion is very familiar with smashing through glass ceilings. Electrified with excitement, she gave me a huge hug as she exclaimed, "How about those women, Silken! How about those women!"

How about them, indeed. I look forward to watching my daughter, stepdaughters and a new generation of women crashing through all the remaining glass ceilings—in sport and everywhere else.

MOVING ON

Maybe I'm naive, but I believe that life will just keep get-ting better. As I shed all the junk that was weighing me down, I find myself stronger and lighter. I am more sure of myself. I am swifter to realize new goals and dreams because I spend far less time spinning in self-doubt or fractured by a crisis of confidence. Although I'm older, I feel like infinitely more things are possible.

When I first started the work of healing, I wanted to be transformed instantly. After I grew trusting of the process, my attitude was "Bring it on!" I wanted to identify a prob-lem, solve it, then move forward at a lightning pace, leaving behind all that was unwanted. Now I realize you can't hurry emotional growth any more than you can suddenly become an Olympic rower. I liken the process to learning to breathe with intention. First you inhale, allowing the oxygen to fill your lungs, then you allow the oxygen to reach your blood cells, then you allow the benefits of that oxygen to work their way through your whole body. There is a lot of "allowing" in healing, just as there is in breathwork. We may begin by allowing ourselves to be consciously aware of an emotional response in our counsellor's office. Then, when we are confronted by that same emotion in our daily lives, we are no longer taken by surprise or feel so completely caught in its grip. We go back to what we learned during counselling, with that lesson now clarified by personal experience so that our awareness resonates a little more deeply, leaving us with a sense of "Hmm, maybe there is something to this."

I used to be embarrassed to admit that I went to a counsellor. I felt ashamed that even though I had so much going for me, I was still struggling. I didn't understand that seeking help is a healthy commitment to mental and spiritual development. Even people close to me sometimes wonder why I still go to see Neil, and if I really need to take anti-anxiety medication—and if too much looking inward becomes the problem in itself. For all the years of wise counselling, I'm truly grateful, and I'll continue on this journey for as long as I feel that working with another person increases my self-awareness, promotes healing and helps me to live a deeper life. I plan to exercise my body throughout all my years to come; why would I not invest as readily in my mind, my emotions and my spirit? I also consider this self-knowledge to be something I pass on, because as I learn, I share through my speaking, my writing and, most recently, my life coaching.

In the work of healing through awareness, I find keeping a journal to be an immensely powerful tool of self-discovery, preventing counselling from becoming too intellectual. By opening myself up to writing, writing, writing whatever bursts forth, without editing, without analyzing, without judging— just dumping it all out on the page—I can bypass my head and see what's in my heart. This also allows me to observe what may be triggering negative emotions and forewarns me if I'm stretching myself too thin.

Even with therapy and medication, I'm still not entirely immune from depression. I can feel it coming on like a grey cloud of sadness and apathy that hangs over me without seeming to have a direct source. It almost doesn't matter what the outer world shows me. It is how I feel about myself right then, at that moment. I no longer try to shut out this clog of pain, to shove it back inside. I allow myself to experience what I am feeling, even if it's inconvenient, uncomfortable and embarrassing. This, too, is part of my journey—my quest for authenticity.

It's always disappointing to me when that sadness, or some external event, opens me up to the nasty belittling voice I still carry in my head. The spark could be my failure to get a particular writing job, or a mean remark somebody made about me, or something inappropriate that I blurted. The difference is that I'm more empowered to stop that voice, or at least to shorten the amount of time it's free to nag me. I now know that I can't blame this on anyone else. It's my own voice parroting back all those untruths hurled at me so long ago. More often now, however, I can speak to myself in the language of caring and compassion. I can even trigger my sense of humour, enabling me to love my perfect imperfect self.

I've also learned another life lesson from my depression: I don't have to suffer in isolation as if living on an island. I can reach out for support. Kim and a few other friends who love me without judgment have become a circle with whom I can candidly share, deepening our relationship by allowing them to support me. There is power in being "with" rather than brooding all alone. This is something new that I had to learn to master.

My urgency to become the best person I can be as quickly as possible is most pressing when dealing with my children. They are growing so fast that I feel I must get over any irrational rage I have *now* so that I will never again yell at them. I will never again make them cry to satisfy something unresolved in my own psyche.

Not long ago, when I was parking our powerboat for the very first time with friends aboard, my daughter yelled instructions, my partner yelled instructions and then my son repeated the instructions the other two were yelling. My daughter was closest to me, and I snapped at her, though she had actually said the least of anybody. That incident ruined my whole morning, not because I scratched the boat but because I had been bad-tempered, once again triggering my cycle of self-doubt and self-dislike. This is where self-forgiveness comes in. If I lose my temper, then spend the next four hours beating myself up or attempting to compensate to my kids out of guilt, I become an inconsistent parent. Better by far to take a few deep breaths, to acknowledge to myself my behaviour, to apologize where necessary, to forgive myself and then to move on. This last involves reminding myself that I am a human being who makes mistakes, and that if I can learn something worthwhile during the process, then that's more important than the error.

I believe that parents must be role models for their kids. They watch what we do, how we live our lives and how we prioritize our time. We can talk to them about loving themselves, but they learn more effectively by seeing us love and honour ourselves at the same time as we love and honour them.

Many of my friends now have adult children, and I think it must be great seeing how they have turned out. What a relief to know they didn't become serial killers or drug addicts! It's a special bonus when your kids have a strong relationship with you in adulthood. My greatest fear used to be that my kids wouldn't love me. I couldn't bear the thought of having the same kind of relationship with them that I have with my mom. It was a nightmare that I played over and over in my head: how my children would reject me, how they would cut me out of their lives. My mom would say that I deserved this, and some part of me would agree.

I now understand that I am not my mom. I have a profoundly different relationship with my children than my mom ever had with me. My kids run home to tell me what they did that day. They tell me that they love me. They tell me what's bothering them. They trust me to protect them from harm.

As the years go by, I find myself understanding bits and pieces of my parents' perspective in the oddest way. When I look at my relationship with Kate and Will, I almost feel that my kids are lucky to have a mother who adores them so much that she would stand in front of a train to protect them. Sometimes I want to tell them this, but how would that make any sense when they have always felt the radiating love of their parents? My kids have no context for that kind of "lucky." So when they have come to me with one of their problems or a perceived injustice, I want to minimize it—to tell them they don't know how lucky they are. And then I catch myself—this is just a different version of what my parents said to me so hurtfully so many times. So I button my lip and try to grow a little—both in how I relate to my kids and how I understand my mom.

*   *   *

Recently, I had a breakthrough in my relationship with my mom. Nothing at all changed in her. The change happened inside me.

Last September, she and Janis visited me in Victoria for ten days. Upon their departure, I wrote the following in my journal:

"I keep turning to my mom when my inner child needs comfort and love. My draw to her is as ancient and primal as breath itself. Even though I know she is not a safe place to hold me, I find myself reaching for her, wanting to fall into her bosom and simply to let go. My mom never was, and will never be, that safe place for me to rest. This was driven home to me during these last ten days, when it became so very clear, yet again, that she simply can't give me the emotional verification I want from her. My mom, despite her abusive anger, is also a perfect child of God; she is also held and treasured, and her greatest journey may well be in her next lifetime. Recently, though, I've discovered that I can find solace in the mother within me. I can ask my inner child what she needs, why she feels lonely, how I can help her. I have the power to listen, and when I step away from ego and judgment, I am able to give her exactly what she requires. This knowing is such a relief. Little Silken will always be loved and safe.

"With this, I am freed. I am freed to redirect my energy

from protecting a child who is not complete, and to create whatever I wish to create. Today, as I write, I realize I have so much more to contribute. I feel my heart fill with energy and life. Forgiveness washes over me. Forgiveness toward anybody who couldn't be what I wanted them to be, but mostly self-forgiveness. Forgiveness for not being what my mom needed. Forgiveness for the fact that I am only human, and for the many mistakes I have made. Forgiveness toward little Silken, who withstood so much painful anguish, and who then spent a lifetime punishing herself for being less than perfect. It becomes self-evident—I am perfect, we all are, we are each a perfect child of God. I connect to the goddess within me. Just as she is everywhere, she is within me. She has been there the entire time—I have been drawing on her strength and wisdom for always.

"It is a spiritual homecoming to arrive at this place. I discover what I have always known: that I am held and treasured as part of a greater force, as surely as each breath I take and as the earth I stand upon.

"It is time to step up again."

*   *   *

As well as parents being role models for their children, I believe that children can serve as role models for their parents. My daughter, Kate, knows she is beautiful. I see this in the confident way she moves and dresses and interacts with people. At age twelve, she has never said one negative thing about her body to me. When we go shopping together, she knows immediately whether something looks good on her. She will twirl in front of the mirror, admiring the fabric, or the cut, or the design with an amazing sense of objectivity and joy. I also marvel at how much she likes just being a girl. She will try different hairstyles, play with makeup, experiment with high heels, completely comfortable with her femininity. I love this about my daughter. She possesses a very strong sense of who she is and what makes her unique and special.

On one shopping trip with Kate, during which I was trying on clothes, she couldn't figure out why I was in such a bad mood. As I fought my way out of a too-tight blouse and flung it onto the floor, my daughter protested, "But that looked so pretty."

Her honest delight in the colours and styles I'd been trying on propelled me to shift my outlook from the grumpy perspective of a mother who now needs a size ten instead of a size eight to the carefree perspective of a daughter having fun helping her mother find a new outfit. The next time I looked in the mirror, I chose to see a healthy woman who'd been gifted with good genetics and who had a tremendous amount of joy in her life. I told my image that I was beautiful, then carefully picked up the blouse I'd flung to the floor. After admiring the colour and fabric, I poked my head out of the change room to ask the sales clerk for a larger size, which I bought.

I've tried to make that image of me a part of every minute of my life, but I know that I still don't see myself as others see me. After examining a recent painting of Kate and me, I told the artist that I couldn't believe how perfectly he had captured Kate. Though I couldn't recognize myself in the painting, my daughter insisted that it was a perfect image of me, too.

I wish I could say I was always totally at peace with my

body, but that wouldn't be true. Love for my body—a feeling everyone deserves to have—is fleeting. More accurately, I would call it a truce, meaning that when I find myself feeling fat, big or old, I dismiss such thoughts as destructive. I consciously choose not to obsess, and I refuse to fuel them by staring at myself in the mirror. If you see me someday with my makeup on unevenly or my hair unkempt, you'll know this was one of those days when I chose not to look.

It's so often my appearance that is the trigger for my crazy self-doubts, yet I know the underlying cause is my deep-rooted feeling of not being good enough, of being worthless and of not belonging. It's not our bodies that need to be changed but our minds. It's the stories we tell ourselves about our value, our goodness, our place in the world. If each of us spoke to our reflection in the language of sweetness and self-love, we would know that we are perfect just the way we are. If we learned to see ourselves with the same delightful eye with which we admire our children, we would love ourselves too much to trust a surgeon's tools to change what we don't like.

I *am* improving. When I was in my twenties and thirties, I had no sense that I was the kind of woman men would find attractive. It wasn't that I thought I was ugly, just that I felt I was missing that *wow!* factor. It took until I was divorced and in my forties for me to begin to feel comfortable in my own skin and to become aware, not in a conceited way, that when I add confidence to my big physical presence, then I *am* beautiful.

I've also learned never to address my body in pieces, such as saying, "I love my arms, but I hate my stomach." My body—all of it—is my constant companion. It allowed me to fulfill my Olympic dreams and to create little miracles inside me. It exists as a whole and must not be separated into pieces. Years after my accident, when I was working with a physiotherapist, he asked me to welcome my leg back into my body. I realized then that after separating it in order to cajole and coax it to heal, I had not reintegrated it. At his suggestion, I drew deep breaths into the tissue and allowed a feeling of peace to pass through my whole being as I visualized my leg rejoining my body in completeness. My body is a sacred place where my soul lives. Now, when I walk around Elk Lake, I consciously listen to my body, whispering my gratitude for its patience in remaining my loyal friend.

I'm still taunted by my eating disorder. When I fall into my "not eating" trap, I feel more in control, even more relaxed and more pleased with my image and myself, just like an alcoholic in the glow of that stolen first drink. The problem is, I know what I'm doing is not healthy. Like the alcoholic, I could well hit a point where I spiral downward. I also fear that if that should happen, I might infect the girls. Conversely, when I'm eating, even if it's a healthy diet, I feel less good about myself, and I want to stop eating to regain that false sense of control. Anorexia is an illness running contrary to common sense. It is also—and here's where the addiction comes in—a coping device that feels to me like an old friend, something to comfort me when I'm stressed. I don't really want to give it up, even knowing I must, because it feels so good when I am otherwise feeling bad about myself. It's weird, I know, but it's this weirdness—this sense of having a special relationship with the way I eat—that makes it so seductive.

Thanks to the help of my counsellor and a few close friends

to whom I confided my problem, I've made the transition to functional eating. I no longer encourage an obsession with fatness or thinness by constantly weighing myself—in fact, I don't even own a scale. I'm still well-toned from working out every day, but I'm not muscle-bound. My body feels looser, more limber, and while I weigh more than I did at the peak of my athletic abilities, I also love myself more. My jeans still fit, but they are tighter in places where they used to be loose, and looser in places where they used to be tight. I wear my hair long and a little wild. I have dumped my workout clothes for a more classic but individual look. I wear good jeans and well-cut jackets and prominent jewellery. I don't try to hide the permanent gouge in my leg from where my flesh was torn apart that fateful day in Essen.

Recently, as I was putting on a pair of high heels and snug jeans—totally new fashion developments for me—my sister said to me, "You are becoming more and more like Mom." Although I bristled at her words, I knew she was right and I was okay with owning this small part of my mom's influence. So here I am at forty-eight, just like my mom, having fun with fashion and becoming excited about finding a flattering new outfit.

★　★　★

I've learned many of my most valuable life lessons from sports, and one of the first was how to set goals and to have dreams. I remember as an adolescent sitting down with my first track coach and talking about our plans for the summer—what times I should achieve to become competitive and how to go about this. What I learned was that hard work and focus lead to success in a concrete and definable way. That connection has made a lasting impression. I begin each new year by writing down what I'm planning for the months ahead, followed by concrete steps toward those dreams. Putting the two side by side ensures that I am investing in actions that move me forward.

Goals and dreams are interconnected. Dreams are what we imagine—visions of the future that excite us at a cellular level. To fulfill these dreams, we must learn the skill of setting both short- and long-term goals. A plan, however naive, is a powerful tool.

When I starting rowing, my short-term goal was to make the National Team in my first attempt. My long-term dream was to become the fastest woman rower in the world. I achieved the short-term goal in a matter of months. The long-term dream took nine years.

This principle of having dreams and setting goals is one that I apply to every aspect of my life. Because I know my mind is powerful, I take time to envision clearly not just what I want but what I consider worthy of pursuit. If I hold that image specifically enough and constantly enough, I have discovered that my imaginings become reality. I also know that a dream appears differently once it materializes. A dream has an idyllic quality, but the actualization of that dream often requires a great deal of hard work over considerable time, possibly hindered by disappointments, making it seem less like a dream and more like a goal. The closer we get to realizing the dream, the more steps we may have taken, so that the last one seems just like one more goal. By the time we are actually living the dream we imagined, say, a decade ago, it may be so completely grounded that we have forgotten its idyllic beginnings.

Setting short-term goals for my speaking career not only kept me motivated but also immersed me in a self-directed course of lifelong learning. Whether the goal was attending a workshop, or attracting ten new clients, or developing a different presentation, all of these moved me closer to my dream of being able to support myself and my children through a career in public speaking.

My dream of becoming a writer began when I was eleven and had experienced terrible trouble reading. It was ignited as a teenager at INDEC, the Independent Education Centre, when I was inspired by plays and ideas. It continued throughout university, after I gave up the dream of becoming a marine biologist, which didn't suit my talents, to study English literature. After my Barcelona win, I began writing inspirational articles and speeches, but it wasn't until 2006, at age forty-one, when I published *Child's Play*, that I allowed myself to say, *I am a writer.*

With most dreams, there isn't a singular moment, like holding your book in your hands or mounting a podium for a medal, that signifies, *Yes, I am living the Dream!* We just become better at what we've chosen to do. With me, it's often only after the fact, when I take a moment to marvel at what has happened, that I realize, *Hey, this is what I dreamed about.* I owned a property on the ocean for quite some time before I stopped and said to myself, *I have a home on the ocean!* This was something I had visualized my entire life. I remember as a teenager talking with my sister about our dream homes. I can look back through my journals and find it mentioned there. While my house looks different from the one on a cliff that I pictured, the feelings and sensations I have about it are the same—the sweep of wilderness, the sound of the wind blowing through the grass, the saltwater waves whipping and cresting.

My dreams are always drenched with feelings. When one comes true, I can forever afterward experience that place in my body. I can smell the air; I can remember my emotions. Winning the World Championship in 1991 felt exactly as I had imagined it a thousand times. It was a fairy-tale race, creating a narrative I could relate for years to come—the sheer elation coursing through my body as I sailed across the finish line, later celebrated in exuberant dancing and partying with rowers from around the world. That gold medal was the biggest thrill of my sporting career, one I could savour in my imagination before it happened and in my memory afterward. Winning bronze in Barcelona following my injury garnered far greater international acclaim, but in reality it felt far more complicated than I had imagined it. Relief had not been part of my dream, nor had my utter exhaustion. In the events leading up to Barcelona, I had an awareness that I was living in a dream every day, every practice, so that when the final race produced a win, I was a little dreamed out, only grateful that the last step had been achieved.

Dreams make life so much more thrilling. As children progressing through the school system, we are urged by our teachers and parents to dream big, set goals, then work to accomplish them. Corporations set targets for their employees. Yet when I'm speaking to people of every age and walk of life and I ask them to reflect on their dreams, they reply with looks ranging from blank disconnect to terror.

Sometimes our dreams seek us out, demanding our attention. At other times we must listen for those special moments of contentment that nudge us in a particular direction. I have discovered that sort of joy while raising funds to help kids. I've found it by winding my way into a new yoga position, or while writing for hours on a rainy afternoon. All these experiences give me vital information about what feeds my soul and my intellect, along with where I might have some talent.

I've also discovered, while speaking to groups, that there's a common misconception of what it means to find one's "calling." People normally put it into the context of your career, but to me it is about following your heart and finding your happiness, whether it's through your work or an outside passion. A calling doesn't necessarily come to you in a thunderclap of recognition, either; it can creep up on you in the doing. Although rowing was undoubtedly my calling, I encountered many days and even weeks when I hated going out in the wind and the rain to row yet another kilometre with raw hands. Yet the moments of joy came frequently enough and intensely enough to keep my enthusiasm high.

If we can't find some delight—some feeling of *wow!*—in what we're doing, probably we're not following our true path. Change takes courage, though often we have more flexibility than we realize. I think of change in ten-degree segments. Perhaps all that is needed to invest life with deeper meaning is to open up a ten-degree space by adding mentoring to administrative work or by exploring a fascinating new hobby. While lamenting our failure to find that illusive perfect dream, many of us miss the signposts and humbler goals that already bring us joy in a softer key.

In pursuit of every dream, I have learned that nothing is more powerful than action—any consistent movement in the right direction, even if the steps seem modest. After my horrendous leg injury caused me to lose precious seconds from my rowing speed, I had to focus on incremental improvement. While I may dream of someday publishing a book that will inspire millions, I can find inspiration for myself right now by writing an article about Kilee's grasp of a new word or Kate's eagerness in writing a play. Whenever I find myself looking for the perfect course of action, I know that fear and doubt may be paralyzing me from doing anything at all.

Yes, sometimes in my life I have paused, become stuck, even gone in the wrong direction. Again and again, I have had to reconnect to my sense of inner knowing, which will not be denied. I have tried to stuff it down, tried to convince myself that an easier or shinier course is better, or that I should focus on making money. Again and again the universe has thwarted my misguided attempts to fight my deepest wisdom, and the more my inner voice has been respected, the stronger it has grown.

Risk and fear are closely related. When my children tell me they don't want to try something new, it's usually because they're afraid of looking bad or, worse, finding that they're not good at it. When Kate was seven, I sat in a church bathroom with her for almost an hour while she tried to summon the courage to get up on the stage to perform her piano piece. When I assured her she didn't have to do it, she kept insisting, "But I want to do it, Mommy!" while still not budging from the bathroom cubicle. Finally, minutes before her name was announced, she scurried onto the stage, red-eyed and shaking, then wowed us with a flawless rendition of "Twinkle, Twinkle, Little Star." Kate took a risk that day whether she played or not. If she hadn't performed, it would have been harder for her the next time. Now she plays in musical theatre, runs cross-country races and participates in synchronized swimming on a provincial level.

Each time we overcome fear through action we are stretching our risk muscle. A seventy-year-old friend confided to me that she struggled against the fear that often comes with age by doing every day something that scares her. My friend's choice was often extreme, like riding bareback; for someone else, it might be wearing a bright yellow hat.

I have a belief, vague on details, that goes something like this: Each of our lives is a book already written whose chapters have multiple endings. Depending on the choices we make, a chapter goes in one direction or another, but the book's narrative moves forward with a relentless rhythm and aspects of inevitability. The things we are meant to do appear again and again in our story, until we recognize our responsibility and accept the challenge. No matter how hard we try to avoid them, or back away because we are scared or unwilling, they keep showing up in various incarnations.

* * *

Some of the most dramatic shifts in our lives happen because of setbacks. Who knew all that I would learn from that second in 1992 when a boat crashed into mine, breaking my ankle and ripping my muscles from my shin bone? My split from

John ushered in the most painful, wonderful decade of my life, which I now confidently describe as my time of blossoming. Even though the dream I'd held in my heart for fourteen years ended, in some ways this was also when my real emotional life began. I woke up, not instantly but over the next few years as I began to become who I was really meant to be. The destruction of my life as I knew it created the space for a new life to emerge. In the months directly after John left, I remember feeling amazed that I could become so excited about having dinner with my friends or walking in my first marathon. The script I'd been given had been destroyed. Suddenly, it was up to me alone to decide how I wanted the story of my life to unfold. What dreams had I set aside? What dreams were still short on substance? With whom did I want to share the next chapter of my life?

Transformational experiences often lead to losses in the form of relationships. Some are broken because they were found to be limiting, or because a crisis created a chasm that could not be bridged; others ended when two people, who had once found solace together while travelling on the same road, came to a fork, amicably parted and moved on. In all cases, I appreciate the love, the joy, the adventure and the commitment that was shared, and wish all good fortune to my former friends as they follow their own stars.

As people have moved out of my life, others have moved in. I once felt overwhelmed by the constant presence of strangers; now I find myself seeing the essence in each person and recognizing—in our collective hurts, fears, hopes, joys—our connectiveness as humans. Some days I even feel a desire to hug everyone I meet, to smile, to offer solace in whatever way the moment allows, like an overattentive mom giving love, assurance, a hand up.

My good friend Jane Roos describes each of us as a diamond, radiating thousands and thousands of beams of refracted light. Nobody can know or define someone else entirely. We are all individuals, complex and beautiful. When I see people from this perspective, I find myself becoming more curious, more apt to ask questions and to listen, often exploding the stereotypes with which I've unconsciously branded them by their occupations or first impressions. A few years ago, I found myself chatting with a Toronto taxi driver in his mid-fifties who came across as a friendly, outgoing man. Eventually, he showed me the photo album he kept tucked under his seat. It was filled, page after page, with pictures of remarkable dollhouses in different architectural styles, with furniture to match. This man shared his passion with such excitement that I knew, as we crawled our way through Toronto traffic, he was a happy man.

I find it's when I'm feeling most vulnerable that I have the strongest urge to reach out to strangers and really connect with them in an unexpected way. On those days when I'm afraid one sharp word could reduce me to tears because I feel surrounded by my failures, I've learned that turning outward and revelling in understanding someone else can completely change my outlook and pull me away from that darkness.

* * *

Parenting is a theme I return to often because it's so important to me and to so many others. When my children were young, I felt tremendous guilt if I took time for myself, and I've witnessed that same guilt in my friends. I believed that being a good mother meant putting the needs of my children ahead of my own at all times, but when I did this too success-fully, I turned into a bad-tempered bitch. Mothers hear con-stantly that we need to prioritize time for ourselves, but we have far too many tasks—the housework, the organizing of family activities, the time spent with our partners, the tend-ing to our children's emotional needs—to actually do it. My friends with careers felt guilty about being away from their kids all day. My friends who were full-time wives and moth-ers felt guilty about not contributing to the family income and frustrated about their wasted professional talents. My friends who worked part time felt guilty both ways: about being at work when they were wanted at home, and about being at home when they were wanted at work. Making things worse is women criticizing others for their choices, rather than cele-brating those who've found ways of staying fit mentally, phys-ically and emotionally by taking time to pursue their passions or by contributing to a social cause.

I used to take my personal time as if it were a piece of cake somebody was trying to steal from me. Now I realize that the only person who was threatening to take it from me was me. How much better to come to terms with this concept: *I give to myself this gift of time every day. I celebrate this gift as an important part of what makes me lovable to myself and others.* Metaphorically, I equate this with the nanosecond of rest I learned to build into my rowing power stroke.

Saying yes to me-time almost always means saying no to someone or something else. These days I say no a lot because

I'm learning to prioritize myself. In the past, I came after a long list of others: my kids, my partner, my friends. Now, I try to be honest about what I need and how to meet that need. While I love spending time with my partner, his business trips are not always fulfilling for me, so I say no to them more often than I say yes. Rather than hosting a dinner party for friends, I might suggest meeting at a restaurant. While it's difficult to say no to someone who is raising money for a worthwhile event, I explore more fully both the effectiveness of the event and how my attending will help. I've also learned to be less concerned about how others might judge me based on my choices.

Now that I'm a parent, I understand my mom's need to feed her creativity by having a creative date with herself every few evenings, or on a Sunday afternoon. I love many of the same things as my mom. I love having the house to myself so I can play the piano or listen to classical music as I sit surrounded by a mountain of books. As a kid, I progressed up to grade eight in piano, and now I want to bring that element back into my life. All forms of creativity are emotionally and spiritually healing to me. This doesn't feel optional. I need to spend time with beauty, whether it's in the backyard with nature, going to an art show, listening to music or reading something I find profound. I've even taken up painting as a hobby and an outlet. It is a vital part of what helps me function as a human being. When I am writing or developing ideas for speaking, I know I am in that place beyond self-doubt, dealing out of my strength and my authenticity. When I dream of my future, I feel motivated to create a body of work that translates what I have learned, and continue to learn, in a way that inspires, supports and motivates others. My time to move forward is now. I am coming into my own, embracing my own capabilities and talents. Some of this is connected to my having entered my forties, when the path ahead may prove shorter than the one already travelled. Mostly it has to do with the welcoming of an awakening that is transforming my life.

I believe that the greatest indicator of future success is how you dream about yourself and your abilities. I also believe that the force of love and creation is everywhere and in everything, and I draw upon this power to give me courage, to ground me when I am vibrating too high and to open my heart. I know that this heavenly force has been with me my whole life, a certainty reinforced by my experience in Barcelona. For years, in the moments before going on stage to spend an hour with an audience, I would feel the ground beneath my feet and utter this prayer: "Please give me the wisdom to share with this audience what they most need to hear. Please open my heart to these people."

When I sit down to write, I pray, "Please give me the courage to write what is true. Please give me the grace to write with clarity and humour and compassion. Please give me the strength to keep writing and feeling and caring. Please help me believe in myself, and the importance of this story. Please help me to think less, write more and lead from my heart."

Sometimes I forget to call upon this amazing power, but it is always walking with me, and whenever I stop long enough to breathe it in, its presence fills my soul. I do not go to church. I don't subscribe to an organized religion. I don't try to figure out what this force is, or what it means, or how it fits into other people's beliefs. I just know that this force is everywhere and in everything.

I also draw upon the wisdom of other cultures. Although I don't know much about the teachings of Buddha, a year ago I bought a Buddhist prayer bracelet that I use as a marker every morning for my gratitude prayer. I'm a physical person, and having this little reminder is useful—if I were more daring, I'd tattoo "grateful" on my wrist.

I do believe that, over time, our physical environment profoundly affects our psyche. Now, in my headland home, waking up to water in all its moods makes me feel more present. It calms and restores my soul. This morning, the tide was so high that when I looked out the windows, I couldn't see the front yard, so it was like being on a boat. Last night, we had such a fantastic storm that at ten o'clock, Patch and I had to go down to the dock to secure our boats and bring up the kayaks. The waves were so rough in the gale-force winds that we had to wear lifejackets even on the dock; above us, the sky was so dark and clear that I could see the stars sparkling and cascading as intensely as the water. During each week, I frequently have moments like this, filled with awe and wonder, connecting me with the infinite world of spirit, lifting me out of my daily routine to remind me that we are all a part of something much larger.

POSTSCRIPT

Five years ago I returned to Lake Banyoles, where I won the 1992 bronze Olympic medal—a moment frozen in time in my mind, and the moment people think of when they think of me.

My emotions ran high as I borrowed a single scull from the Banyoles rowing club, then headed out onto the lake, breathing in the silence and the beauty of this once-familiar place. In so many ways, it was just as I remembered—the water tranquil, its smell so sweet and fresh; the clusters of small buildings along the shore; and the sense of being cocooned in my own little world. I remembered the tree under which I often chatted to the media with apparent confidence about the upcoming challenge—and a second tree where I lay crying on the evening before my final race. I remembered the starting area with its three buildings, and the boy who held my boat and took my water bottle. I remembered the ordinary people out for a stroll as if nothing momentous was about to happen, while I awaited the crack of the starting pistol.

As I rowed down the lake, I imagined myself in a centre

lane, recapturing my emotions and the feel of my body on that special day . . . *My legs are driving down against the foot stretchers, fast and hard. My arms are an extension of the oars. My body and the boat are one, held together by my will and the speed of my shell slicing through the water. Though my mind is wiped clear of thought, everything I am—my hurt, my anger, my need for independence, everything that is raw and hungry and unfettered—is behind each stroke. How can something so intense be so lovely? I move powerfully with my lungs squeezing tight and the pressure building in my chest. I exhale forcefully, hoping to push out so much air that I make space for a little more on the next inhale. It hurts, the lactic acid burning hard in my legs, building to a crescendo, so that I want to scream in pain. Instead, I strengthen my attack, feeding off my adrenaline, hammering it out, driving it through—aggression informed by precision and an awareness of how fast the boat is moving, of how hard the water is pushing against it, of how the wind may be unbalancing it, of how the other racers are falling back or gaining.*

As I near the end of the race, I feel an energy surge, and suddenly the finish line doesn't seem so far away. The scoreboard behind the grandstand tells me what I am still too confused to know—that I have won a medal.

My row on that return trip was so quiet—no crazy cheering from the Canadian stands. Gone were the hype and the tension, with my every nerve ending on fire. Gone were the relief and the utter, total, complete, absolute exhaustion. In truth, Banyoles seemed to have grown smaller in the years of our separation, and some of the magic was missing.

As I headed back to shore in the borrowed scull, I remembered how often I had worked on the tiniest pieces of my stroke, and how many bell notes I had rowed alone on lakes, my oar exiting cleanly and crisply. For half an hour I would go around in circles, trying to get that bell sound exactly right.

By the time I returned the borrowed scull, my hands were blistered and my legs tired. One of the Spanish rowers there told me, "I know your story. Everybody knows your story."

I wondered exactly what that story was, how it was told and if it truly reflects what happened that day. I also wondered how my own story had changed through time—the story I told myself, the story I told my kids—and how I might have reinvented and packaged it, altering the truth with what I imagined without realizing it. Yet even after all this time, my story still feels like a miracle—that I was there, that I made it to the finish line despite my injury, that I competed with the best in the world and that I managed to win.

I am grateful to have been in Banyoles those many years ago, and to have made the return journey. Sport is a great illustrator of the power of the mind, the body, the emotions and the role of grace. I am lucky to have experienced all those in the right measure, at the right time.

More importantly, I am grateful that I did not become stuck there, that I moved on to other very special moments, in other very special places, with other very special people. Fame is an outfit that we wear for a while and usually outgrow. We are not defined by any one event, however spectacular or difficult. I no longer row in circles, looking for that perfect stroke. But instead I look ahead to a bright future—one that is as layered and exciting and intense as the past I've finally claimed as my own.

ACKNOWLEDGMENTS

Writing this book has been an emotional start-and-stop project. As I began to consider writing my story, there were several people who were constant in their support and in their conviction that telling it was important. My dear friend Kim Van Bruggen envisioned the book before I did. She believed it would help so many people, and she encouraged me to find the courage to put my experiences and perspectives on the page. My partner in life, Patch, worried about the pain that would accompany the writing of this book; despite this, his support was unwavering. Through the process of writing and publishing my story, we have come to understand and respect each other even more, and for that I am deeply grateful.

There were several times in the writing of this book when I was frozen by fear and doubt. Jane Roos, Bal Arneson, Cam Harvey, Jodi Hosking, Michael Smith, Martine Norris, Fay Melling, Ralph Bruggen, Elizabeth Peckham, Molly and Frank Napolitano, Laurie Anne Faulkner, and Nancy Wardle, you were there for me—sending me emails, pushing me forward and often giving me some needed perspective. My brother, Joerg, gave me support and love two years ago, when I shared with him how open I intended to be in this book.

My brilliant and passionate literary agent, Michael Levine, saw what this book needed before I was able to and encouraged me to bring on Sylvia Fraser to help me with *Unsinkable*. Sylvia, you are a dazzling writer who could see the story from the first day we spoke. You brought your finely honed craft to the project, making a book out of my unstructured mass of writing. My editor, Kate Cassaday, a fellow oarswoman, looked at the book from every angle and made important edits to the manuscript. You brought my voice more clearly into the manuscript and contributed a valuable, fresh perspective.

*   *   *

William and Kate, not only have you listened to me talk about this book, and at times shared my struggles with it, but you have also been born into a family with a public life. It was not your choice to have a mother who shares her life publicly and who has now written such an open book. Your patience in waiting while people talk to me in the grocery store, your maturity in understanding the responsibility I feel in being a public person, and your tolerance of the embarrassment of having other people always recognize your mother—all that is noticed and appreciated. I love you both beyond words.

Laurie De Armond, my assistant of ten years, your caring and listening go far beyond any professional connection. This project, as well as so much else in my life, would not be possible without you.